ALASKA – MY LIFE BEFORE ...
MY LIFE AFTER ... A
TRAVELLER'S STORY

MARK CHENEY

Published 2011 by arima publishing

www.arimapublishing.com

ISBN 978 1 84549 451 3

Printed and bound in the United Kingdom

Typeset in Garamond 11pt

Swirl is an imprint of arima publishing.

arima publishing
ASK House, Northgate Avenue
Bury St Edmunds, Suffolk IP32 6BB
t: (+44) 01284 700321
www.arimapublishing.com

I would like to thank Rosemary for all the help she has given me in writing this book.

CONTENTS

INTRODUCTION

Part one of this book is all about my trip to Alaska, traveling by motorbike, something I have always wanted to do. It documents my journey, my daily chores, the people I meet, the things I get up to…all just wonderful. I want to return as soon as possible, but life has other ideas in store for me…

Part two is about my normal day-to-day life after my trip, when one day, I become the victim of a horrendous accident, which is to leave me fighting for my life…for years I struggle to recover…will I ever straddle a motorbike again?

PART ONE

CHAPTER 1. MY BACKGROUND

I was born in 1943 into a working class family. My parents were both caring and hard working. They always did their best for us all and, although times were hard, we never wanted for food. It wasn't easy bringing up three children but, as the youngest, I was quite spoilt! However, I don't consider my childhood, spent in three villages in the Cotswolds, to have been a particularly happy one - I believe possibly a fault of my own.

Whilst growing up, I took on a paper round which gave me a little money to fulfil one of my dreams - **to own a motorcycle!** One day, when delivering my newspapers, I spotted an old motorcycle in a shed and immediately asked the owner if he would sell it! The cost was £5 - six weeks' wages for me - but, within six weeks, I appeared with the hard-earned cash. I had to push it home, but my dreams of effortless travel had finally materialised. I had a motorbike! I stripped it of every part that wasn't needed. This made it slightly easier for me to push the bike for a mile to the field, where I would ride it around and around until it ran out of petrol! I would then push it all the way back home! I was totally smitten - what fun!

At the age of 15, I started work as an electrician's apprentice. This brought a new sense of freedom for me. My wages were very little, but I was learning a trade. When my apprenticeship was completed, I moved from contract to contract. It was a time of great learning and set me in good stead for the future. Within ten years, I had started my own company, married and had three wonderful children (2 sons and a daughter). This was a very happy time for me, as my children were also my friends and I often took them out on my bike when they had grown enough to enable them to reach the footrests - we all had a great time!

In my youth, my mode of transport was initially a pushbike, but when I reached sixteen I bought a motorbike. It was a 1939 350cc AJS, which met my requirements, until one night I was dazzled by car headlights and I ended up following the bike up the road on my backside. After picking myself up, stuffing the two silencers in the remains of my coat, I picked up the bike and rode home. It wasn't steering very well and, on inspection the next day, I found the frame was bent. I sold it and bought another bike. Although I was never without one, money was tight and the bikes were always old. However, rebuilding bikes enabled me to sell several of them to make enough money for future biking. I always dreamed of travelling the world on a motorbike and would read of adventurous people who crossed the channel and toured the continent.

My motorcycling changed when I bought my first BMW with a self-starter. This was the R90S, a sports tourer. Finally, I had the bike to allow me to venture further afield. I started travelling, sometimes with one of my children, but mainly on my own. I would always ask my wife to come with me "come just once and you'll love it", but the reply was always the same "No". She once told me to go and get it out of my system. This, I have since found, is impossible - you never do! My wife and I parted at the age of 47. My travelling continued and I covered many European countries, again mainly alone, but I always had great experiences and wonderful times. "Get it out of your system" - not a chance!!

CHAPTER 2. I WANT TO DO A BIG BIKING TRIP!

I had a couple of trips in mind. The first was to ride into Russia but, on making enquiries at the time, it was totally out of the question. The country was in turmoil and a lone rider would most certainly not have survived.

In 1997, a trip I had thought about for a long time began to materialise. **Alaska - the last frontier.** It was just phone calls to start with, then the details. What bike would be suitable, taking into account the dirt roads, the bike's carrying capacity and the price? Would it be cheaper to hire a bike or fly one from England to Alaska? Finally, I decided to hire one through a company in Anchorage. I chose a Kawasaki 650cc KLR, complete with panniers and an extremely small rear carrier. Everything I needed would have to be carried on my bike. Food, tent, sleeping bag, bedroll, spare boots and last, but not least, my barbecue, built from my own design by a Wilshire-based company: stainless steel and folding into nothing, ideal for bikers with limited storage. Clothes, leathers and weather proof gear were all packed in a loose bag, small bits, books and maps into a haversack. To enable me to pack all this stuff across the bike with very little effort, I made up a very simple aluminium carrier, just 4 pieces of metal and 4 bolts, attached to the existing carrier with nylon ties.

I have to say that this trip, which was to take four weeks, was made possible because my youngest son, who was now part of my business, was able to manage the company in my absence.

My basic plan was to travel through Alaska, after picking up the bike near Anchorage, via Denali, the arctic circle crossing the Yukon to Dawson. (but this could change as I got into the journey).

The date was set - July - the planning complete and, with just a week to go I started packing my bags, checking and double-checking my lists!

On the morning of my departure I awoke at 6 a.m., up and off to meet the coach which was to take me to Heathrow, where I would change to another coach for Gatwick airport.

At last the coach arrived. Everything was loaded up and away we went. I eventually arrived at Gatwick airport, checked in, had some breakfast and then decided to get through Customs. I calmly strolled up to the scanner, all hell broke loose, alarm bells going off everywhere. Two officers took me to one side and told me to empty my pockets; small change, penknife, whistle, compass, scissors, torch, keys. "OK, walk through again" - off went the alarm bells - then I had the hands-on treatment. "Take your belt off - OK walk through again". Alarm bells yet again. The officers produced this thing, rather like an oversized dildo. I thought "now hang on a minute, where do you intend to stick that thing what were their intentions?" Relief came as they ran it over my person. All was fine until they reached my boots and away it all went again. Off came the boots. After a thorough inspection they handed them back. "it's the nails" they said and promptly told me to move on. I gathered my things up and walked to the departure lounge. Finally, the boarding sign went up. As I walked towards the gate I could see the plane. It wasn't a jumbo, but it was very large with three engines, one on each wing and one on the tail. I boarded and found my seat.

CHAPTER 3.   OK - ALASKA -   HERE I COME!

The flight was OK, as flights go. The first stop was Minneapolis, the twin cities. All I saw was the airport, the departure lounge.

A lady, very loud and stern, seemed to be offering passengers 200 dollars to take the next flight. Since that would take 2 hours off my journey, I thought I would go for that, but as I moved forward, I realised she was actually offering 200 dollars off any flight you took with the airline in the next year!

I eventually headed to the boarding gate, still hanging onto my helmet - not the easiest of things to carry on a plane. I boarded and, great, I had a window seat.

As we were nearing Alaska, the scenery became breath-taking. Mountains and glaciers, a sight to behold. I couldn't take my eyes off the wonder of it all. However, I imagined it to be quite cold, just miles and miles of mountains and snow. WOW!

CHAPTER 4.   ANCHORAGE

Quite late in the evening, we landed in Anchorage, a city that looks like any other city - buildings and more buildings. I took a taxi into town, looking at hotels on the way. They looked nice, but quite expensive. My first stop was the youth hostel. They were full that evening but gave me the name of a sub-letting house. I arrived at rather a nice wooden house, unloaded the gear and paid the taxi driver. After looking around, I found some stairs running up the outside of the building. As I walked up, I found the door was open and looking in, I saw a chap sitting at a large desk. I knocked on the door and introduced myself. "Well, hi there, my name is Jack and I run this establishment. Where have you arrived from today?" "England - I wondered if you have a room for one night", I replied. "Well, you must be tired, come on in and sit down". I did and began to look around.   He was obviously a hunter as his trophies were hanging everywhere. Also I noticed that he had an Indian wife, with just one hand; he waved her out of a chair for me to sit down. I wasn't impressed and must admit I wasn't very taken with Jack, who was taking his time to look at some list. "I think I can fix you up with something. Yes, but you will have to share - it's just round the corner".

Thank the Lord for that, I wouldn't want to stay in his house. He pushed back his chair and asked me what I was doing in Alaska. "Just a holiday" I replied, "I plan to tour around on a motor bike". "Motor bike, oh how wonderful, what a great thing to do. What part are you going to?" "All over" was my reply. "Well how wonderful. No one tours Alaska on a bike". This man was making me feel very uncomfortable and I really couldn't wait to get out of his office but he insisted on telling me about his hunting and how many bears he had killed.   He was so 'modest', indicating he was the best hunter in Alaska! He was also directing his wife with signs. I really did have a bad feeling about him. At last, he directed me to his other house, just a few hundred yards away. I was grateful to be saying goodbye, thank God I was away.

Grabbing my bags, I set off up the road and saw my base for the night, a very dilapidated bungalow. I walked over to find there were two men already there. They introduced themselves as Leroy and Jack. They seemed very nice - they were in Alaska for the fishing. They showed me my room and I dumped my bags.

Having settled in, I remembered I had to phone Tom, the motor cycle dealer. I couldn't use the house phone as I had no telephone card. I decided to ask Jack to ring for me and tell Tom I had arrived and where I was staying. "No" was his answer "there's a pay phone about a quarter of a mile away". Not surprised at this response, I wandered back and Leroy kindly lent me his card and I arranged with Tom to pick me up at 9.30 a.m. the next day.

I sat and chatted with Leroy and Jack. It seemed they would be fishing all summer. They even took me to the river to look at a salmon run. Back to base, I turned in after a long tiring day.

The next morning was bright and sunny and I decided to have a walk to find some breakfast, soon finding a café and ordering a full cooked breakfast and, for the first time, I was asked how I would like my eggs - easy, over easy and so on! After enjoying a great breakfast, I wandered back to the lodgings, arriving just in time to see a large pickup heading my way. Tom, the motor cycle dealer, pulled up and I introduced myself. My bags were loaded into the truck and away we went.

Tom seemed a very amiable chap and we chatted quite freely. Our journey was about an hour long and, leaving the city behind, I began to see Alaska; Mountains in the distance and large forest areas - some sight. Tom was full of information and described a few trips he had done himself.

When we neared the house, I could see the KLR waiting for me. Tom offered to sort out the paperwork whilst I did the packing. First, my carrier. I bolted it together and then fixed it to the small rear carrier with nylon ties. Next, I repacked my 'stuff sack' , which was rather like a very large sausage with a zip. I put it across the new carrier and tied it with bungee. Then I packed the panniers and everything went in with room to spare. I went through my bike gear and set it out, ready to wear. I lashed out at a wasp and as I did this, there was a scream. One of the children went running into the house - yes, a wasp sting, there must be a nest nearby and the noise seemed to bring more to investigate me and my bike! I was continually dodging them. Tom brought me a drink, so I sat under the shade of a tree as it had become quite warm.

With the paperwork out of the way, Tom went through bits of information to do with the bike, i.e. the starting procedure, petrol on and settings, choke, plus small daily jobs, oil and coolant. He then wished me a good holiday and I fired the **big single** up I set off down the drive, went to change into second gear and couldn't find the gear change. I

realised I had my feet on the rear rests - clever!!

.

CHAPTER 5. I SET OFF AT LAST

My first stop would be to buy food and I found a small shopping centre and parked up. First priority - beans, various tinned foods, bread and water. While shopping, I noticed a closing down sale and bought myself a pair of binoculars at a very reasonable price. This proved to be a success story as I used them so much. In fact, never go to Alaska without a pair of binoculars! I fired up the big single and away, through Wasilla on the road to Talkeetna. These roads are quite busy but, at the same time, run through quite pleasant countryside. It was nearing lunch time so I started looking for a roadside café. Soon I found one. It didn't look that good but, being hungry was enough to get me in there. I had chilli and a beer - it went down very well.

After lunch, I was on my way again and, although I wasn't too happy with the vibration coming through the handlebars on my bike, it was running well. There was quite a magnificent view of Mount McKinley - the locals call it Denali. I pulled over and got some wonderful pictures, with McKinley filling the skyline. Just as evening closed in, I arrived at Talkeetna, a town from the past, just one street with a few shops, bars and boarding houses. I decided to find a roadhouse, the American boarding house. I parked my bike and was viewing the prices when the owner approached me and asked if I would like a room. "A little too much money" I told her. She offered to reduce the price and introduced herself as Tricia. She showed me the room and then the bathroom. Wow, this was just the sort you would normally see in cowboy films! Was I supposed to keep my gun under the pillow in case anyone walked in and then just let them have it?! I had a bath and a nap and then it was time for dinner.

I struck up a conversation with George, the cook, who said he had once been the cook for George Bush Senior, the ex-President of America. George (not the president!!) spends his life cooking during the summer, whilst looking after his dogs at night. During the winter, he is a musher (he drives a husky dog-drawn sleigh racing across the wilderness).

The dogs have to be well looked after and maintained at peak fitness for their hard life pulling the sleigh. They have to travel hundreds of miles. This was something I knew very little about and now I was gaining knowledge first hand. Apparently, it costs a lot of money, but if you make it, there are sponsors and prize money to help. George's laugh was something else! I found him very interesting and we chatted for an hour. There were plans to go to the Fairview Inn after dinner for a dance and I was invited along.

The Fairview was just up the street, a saloon just like those I had seen in films. It was wonderful, made entirely of wood and it seemed to have been there for ever. I found it very welcoming and to my pleasure they had Guinness. I had my drink and was sitting down taking in the atmosphere, when I noticed a chap walk up to the bar. He looked a bit like "Doc Holiday" from the old western films. He was wearing a sort of three quarter length suit. He ordered his drink and then he lent back on the bar and as he did this, his coat opened and there, strapped to his waist, were two 45 colts in very nice holsters!! Wow! This was a bit of a surprise for me, a country lad, to take in. I sat for a while, trying not to let him see me looking at him, but I couldn't take my eyes off him. He downed his drink, wished the barman farewell and left. Well, unable to contain myself, I went to the bar and asked who the chap was who had just left. "Oh, that's our local Doctor". I thought to myself "well I've not seen one like that back home"!!

After this episode with "Doc Holiday", Tricia, my landlady, came over and asked me if I could dance. I told her I could jive and she reckoned she could, but was not very good. Well, that wasn't a problem since I can lead, as long as I have the right rhythm before I start. Within a short time, on came the right stuff. Once I picked up the beat, we cleared the floor and danced the night away!!

I awoke to the sun streaming through the window and went down to my bike. To solve the vibration problem I acquired some very thin foam to wrap around the two handle grips. It didn't look good, but it would do the job.

CHAPTER 6.   MOUNT McKINLEY

Before I left Talkeetna, I wanted to try a flight around Mount McKinley. I found the flight office, and they could get me on a flight almost straight away so I walked to the airfield. The flight was due in about ten minutes. The lady from the office walked to a very small plane parked on the edge of the runway. She had what I would call the bonnet up and was fiddling around. After that, she put the fuel in it. I watched her with great interest and wondered whether she was the pilot as well. She ran back to the office and told me the plane was ready to go. I was just about to walk to the plane, when a very large car pulled up alongside. Three people stepped out, an elderly couple and a younger woman, probably their daughter. At the same time, another chap appeared. The office, petrol and mechanic lady introduced him as the pilot. He asked our names and told us to please make our way to the plane. I was told to get in the front to be strapped in. The daughter started kicking up a fuss - "I was led to believe that we would have the plane to ourselves, not sharing with anyone else". Oops, that someone being me. I wondered whether they realised I was from England?! The pilot was very polite and told them they were only able to fly with four people as it would be totally uneconomical to do otherwise. They moaned and groaned and created a very uncomfortable atmosphere. In fact, their outburst put a bit of a dampener on the whole trip.

Somehow they managed to strap us all in and the pilot started to turn the engine over. It seemed very slow but then all hell broke loose. At the same time as it fired up, it threw out a cloud of smoke, rattled and rolled and shook! Was this really a good idea? We started rolling, the pilot revved it up and the next minute we were racing down the runway. I wondered whether it would ever get off the ground, but when I next opened my eyes, we were skimming over the tops of the trees - only just. The pilot headed towards the mountain and was saying something, but I couldn't hear him. My headset didn't seem to be working, so I spent the whole of the trip in my own little world. I settled down and started to enjoy it.

The plane seemed to catch a gust of wind at one point, rolling and then righting itself again. Oh, I really hoped my breakfast would stay down, I really didn't feel too good. After this roll, one of many, I looked ahead. The clouds were coming down fast, so I wondered whether the pilot would turn back, but he announced that he would fly up the approach to the passes as far as the clouds and then turn around. What a turn. It seemed too narrow, but he managed it. On we went, doing about ten more passes, by which time I was having difficulty hanging onto my breakfast, which seemed a lot nearer the surface, ooooooh Lord. It would have been magnificent if I had been feeling a little better!

At last we turned for home and at the same time went into a dive to look at a moose. Finally, the landing strip appeared and I opened my eyes as we were coming to a halt outside the hanger. I thanked the pilot for a wonderful trip, jumped out and ran to the toilet. I did find him later when I was feeling a little better, had a chat and gave him a tip. I must be mad! However, I think I will always remember my flight and Mount McKinley.

After the flight, the sun was shining, so I took a leisurely walk towards the town, beginning to feel a little better! As I approached the railway line, I saw a train approaching the crossing from my right. Well, what a train. The biggest one I had ever seen. Some of the carriages had sunroofs but it also had goods wagons as well - it was so long it took ages to pass by. I took a few photos - I was really into my dream trip now.

I returned to my boarding house, quite pleased with my morning's activities. I thought I would take a little ride on the bike for the rest of the afternoon, so gear on and away. I took all the little tracks I could find. I found many houses in the most isolated places but, having said that, they were more like shacks than houses, hardly good enough to live in. I came across a 'teepee' at the end of one of the tracks and, as there was no one around, I was able to get some good photos.

Moving on a bit, I came upon another shack. It wasn't just a shack on its own - there were dumped old cars, falling-down sheds, and rubbish all over the place. I thought "must get a picture of this lot". I stopped my engine and was setting my camera up when a chap appeared. I recognised him from the pub the night before. I opened my mouth to greet him, then realised he was carrying a shotgun and he was telling me to "f…k off and don't come back". Oh crikey! I very quickly stashed the camera , climbed on my bike, ignition on……engine wouldn't start! I realised I must have hit the 'kill' button, so I tried it again and it fired up. Thank goodness for that - I took off like a scalded cat - and didn't look back! I was relieved to find the main road again and I drifted along, taking in the scenery and thanking my lucky stars the bike started!! It also dawned on me that the handle bar vibration had gone - the foam must be working.

I decided to venture down another track and stumbled across a chap working on log cabins - lots of them. So, I parked the bike and walked over to him. He was very interesting and said he builds cabins then transports them to wherever people want them. I had a conducted tour around a small house that was finished - I decided they would be O.K. if you lived in Alaska, but couldn't see myself taking one home!

I rode back into town, stopped at the pub for a pint and a bowl of soup, deciding what to do next.

Talkeetna was nice, but it was time to move on. I set off and was soon riding on tarmac roads again. Once my bike had warmed up, I settled down and listened to the big single talking to me.

I pushed on: my plan was to reach the Denali Highway. After two hours of riding, I pulled in for fuel and met a couple of bikers - with back up - their wives were in a R.V. (recreation vehicle), or as they say in the 'lower 48' (the rest of America!) a large house on wheels. These R.Vs have every kind of refinement one could ever wish to have. They are purpose-built and apparently aimed mainly at the American adventurer. Unbelievably, some R.Vs are similar in size to British coaches and some are even designed to tow cars. They are so self-contained, they can travel hundreds of miles requiring stops only for fuel. More commonly, the Americans travel in 4-wheel vehicles similar to the British Range Rover.

How could these modern American adventurers ever be related to the early pioneers?! Anyway, these bikers seemed very nice and gave me good information regarding the dirt road I was about to encounter. Apparently, they had travelled the area many times, mainly before they were married. They knew the Denali Highway well and gave me a few tips and some possible places to camp

My plan was to continue along the road for three miles and take a left turn onto the old Denali Highway. I straddled the single and pushed off, For a short while I was on tarmacadam and then dirt. The big KLR started talking to me. The scenery, once again, was wonderful and really too much to take in.

This continued for about 50 miles with not another soul on the road. Finally, there was a sign for a roadhouse, which I hadn't seen in the Milepost (the traveller's bible of Alaska). I pulled in and parked the bike near the road. Looking at myself, I noticed I was covered in dust from head to toe. I tried brushing it off, to no avail.

I wandered up the steps to the open door and looking in I saw a bar, with beer! There was a chap who had obviously heard my bike arrive and was waiting for me. I wished him "Good evening" and asked for a beer. He was the owner, but he actually lived in Anchorage. He fed me a lot of information on his numerous achievements, flavoured with a considerable amount of bullshit!

In the background, I noticed an extremely attractive girl moving about the kitchen with another man. After a while, the couple appeared from the kitchen and we exchanged greetings. I said "if bullshit were money, your boss would make a fortune". That made them laugh. Obviously they were of the same opinion. Once we had all picked ourselves up, they introduced themselves. They were Dutch and had been cycling around Alaska. They had run out of money so had taken a job looking after the roadhouse, finding the owner very hard to get on with and hoping to move on as soon as possible. There was also Anton, another Dutchman, spending a short holiday with them. We proceeded to have another beer, chatting quite happily. It was nice to see Europeans again.

Soon after, two R.Vs rolled into the car park and two elderly couples emerged. Quite an intense conversation took place, with a great many hand gestures. The women were wearing strange hats - I wondered whether they were Mormon or part of some sort of religious sect. They appeared to select a spokesman and dispatched him towards the door. We were all quite amused watching this. Anton told us to get ready and as the door slowly opened, complete silence fell. The man walked in and we wished him a hearty "good evening". His head dropped, but there was no reply. There was a long silence as we all waited for some sort of communication. Eventually he barked "rooms?"

After a long pause, he asked what the rooms were like and Anton offered to show them to him. I couldn't look at the others, since I was concentrating too hard on not laughing out loud. As soon as they left, we were all chuckling. On their return, silence prevailed again. Out of the blue, the man asked whether spare sheets were provided! A few more questions followed, with prolonged pauses between each one. "What time can we go into the room? What time will breakfast be?" etc….. After another long pause, he told us he'd be back in a few minutes. He moved slowly out of the door and down the path to meet his associates. There followed a very intense conversation, many hands and arms were waving and fingers pointing in our direction.

Next thing we knew, the old girls were on their way. I leapt over the bar as everyone else disappeared. We quickly reassembled as one of them reached the door. She looked quite frightening and I wondered where she had parked her broomstick! I heard someone say "fancy waking up with her on the pillow". It was fast turning into a comedy. However, as her hand went to the door, there was complete silence. No wonder the man looked so miserable. I'm sure I would if she was with me!! It took another fifteen minutes before they made the decision to stay - but that wasn't all. They wanted the other couple to be able to park up for the night and use all the facilities, inclusive in the price! When Anton agreed, they finally disappeared.

The weather was still looking good and it was time to move on and look for a camping place in the hills. I said my farewell and declined the offer to stay the night. I had really enjoyed my visit, but now needed to move on. I fired up the big single and continued into the night with good light, as night time was only a brief two hours and even that was twilight. I planned to cover about thirty-five miles to a large bridge over the river Susitna. After that, I was to turn left into the hills, towards the Old Denali mining camp. It seemed like no time at all to reach the bridge. I couldn't slow down as the bridge was made out of wood, so I just kept the power on and flew across. Turning onto the old mining road, I reduced my speed considerably to enjoy the hilly scenery. After a couple of miles, there was an abandoned car. I stopped as I hoped there would be a number plate on it, which said "the last frontier". No number plate and not much metal - the vehicle was just shot to pieces and was riddled with holes. I had never seen anything like it; there were more bullet holes than car. I was soon back on the bike, drifting along the tracks and, rounding a corner I saw what at first I thought was a fox which ran across the track in front of me. As I drew closer, I realised it was a porcupine. As a Cotswold's lad I knew all about these: do not get him rattled or get too close. I watched it for a while whilst it lolloped about and made its way down the bank to finally disappear out of view.

CHAPTER 7. FIRST CAMP: "MOOSE DROPPINGS" CAMP

Thrilled with having just witnessed a porcupine, I moved on through some wonderful countryside, down a hill and over a bridge. I started to climb the other side, when I noticed a lady to my right. It looked to me like she was panning for gold. She looked up and waved. I returned the wave and   pushed on towards the old gold mining area. The track got narrower and narrower until I was riding up a stream.   Alongside, I noticed a nice flat elevated area and I pulled the bike over decided this would be my first camp.

I soon had the tent up and sealed the mosquito net as there were a great many mosquitoes about. I got the anti-mosquito spray out and gave my scarf, hat, neckband, balaclava and headband a good spray.   The headband was bought in Holland on the recommendation of a biker friend and it proved very useful. It was a good scarf for biking and could be made into a hat to keep the bugs off my head during the evenings. I ate a dinner of beans, some sort of meat, bread and butter and afterwards had a wander around the area and with disbelief I noticed there were moose droppings everywhere. "Shit", I thought! It certainly looked as if a great many moose had grazed this area recently.   Fortunately, looking around, there were none to be seen. They can be quite large and could easily make mincemeat of a chap. Using my binoculars, I still couldn't see any moose and I hoped they had moved on to another area. I decided that I would name each camp, so this was to be "Moose Droppings" camp. These droppings are small and egg-shaped, about the size of an olive. I later found out that the local Indians collect them, dry them out and varnish them to make earrings and necklaces

After a good night's sleep, the first thing I noticed the next morning was a mosquito bite on my hand, oh dear, be careful. After cleaning my teeth using the water bottle - any of the streams can carry infections deposited by animals - I wandered up the stream in my motorcycle boots. My BMW dealer at home told me these boots never leak. I found they actually do, but I doubt one is supposed to walk in water with them!

The sun appeared to be reflecting off many shiny bits in the water. Could it be gold? On closer inspection, I decided it was fool's gold. I walked back to the camp, dropped the tent, stowed all my bits and tied it all on No rush, as I like to make a leisurely start and slowly build up to ride a little faster if need be as the day goes on. I tend to drift a little and have a good look around the camping area to pick up any rubbish. All seemed well when I fired up the big KLR and checked it over. I set off down the stream, onto the track and away.

When I crossed the bridge, there was that lady again. She certainly was panning. She waved, so I pulled over, parked my bike and walked towards her. As she turned to greet me, I noticed her very big dog and I stopped in my tracks. She greeted me with a warm smile and told me not to worry about her dog as he was a big softy, a husky-cross, very appropriately named Ben. Her name was Jane and she was a nurse in Anchorage, now spending two weeks of her holidays panning for gold. Her friend and protection was Ben - and a gun. She had a tent and a pickup truck. From our initial conversation, she struck me as being a very independent lady. She was also extremely interesting and knowledgeable. When I told her about the gold I had found this morning, she smiled and said I was right, it was fool's gold. She asked me whether I would like to do some panning, which I certainly did. Off came my gear and after a little instruction, I had my head down. My glasses were essential, the flecks of gold were so small that the only way I could see them was with my reading glasses on. The roar of the water made conventional conversation very difficult, but we managed with sign language and shouting. This carried on for some time. The there was an 'explosion' - I found my first ever gold. Jane was thrilled for me. The gold I found then I still have now - untold wealth! Over the next two hours, I also went on to find garnets. Jane told me that she usually made enough on the gold she found to pay her way for the two weeks she was on holiday. We sat with a cup of tea and a sandwich and chatted about my home and life and Jane's life.

However, once lunch was over, I decided to be on my way. I had enjoyed this experience very much and I gave Jane my key-ring from the Isle of Man TT races. She told me she would be back in Anchorage by the time I was there in a month's time and told me to ring her.

CHAPTER 8. STOPOVER AT TANGLE RIVER INN

I straddled the big single and fired it up. With a wave I was away - riding once again was great. Having never ridden on dirt, I must say I was enjoying it, pushing on hard. The KLR was talking to me and, in no time, I was riding by the seat of my pants.

There was very little traffic, just the odd RV. I finally got off the dirt onto tarmac roads and, pushing on, I could see numerous dark clouds ahead, approaching Tangle and Tangle Lakes. Fuel was running low but, from my Milepost manual, I knew I could make it to Tangle. There was a very large roadhouse up ahead, the Tangle River Inn, with fuel on site, so I rolled in and filled up, at the same time observing the increasingly dark rain clouds. Something was coming and boy, did it rain. Looking at the weather, I decided to stay. The room was ok, rather like a portacabin.but it was warm and cosy. There was a shower block, so I took myself off to have a shower, a good shave and a general brush-up.

At the restaurant, there were garments, with very attractive markings, on display, apparently designed by one of the cooks, who I met later that evening - a bought a couple, then, realising I would need to post them back to UK as no room in my bag I would have to find a Post Office!. After I ordered a beer and my meal, I had a good look around. It was an enormous log cabin, very tastefully decorated. Once my dinner arrived, the waitress started chatting. As I was English, she couldn't wait to tell me all about her life. She had one son, who was currently living with her ex-husband in the lower 48. Apparently, when she was married, she had asked her husband if he would help her buy a horse. He had refused and told her that if she wanted a horse, she had to get a job and work for it. Within a week she had found a job and left him, ending up in Tangle, Alaska, with her sister, the cook, and a friend. She is now the proud owner of a horse and rides it every day. I was really enjoying my evening, but it was time for bed.

After another wonderful night's sleep, I crawled out of bed to have a shower. As it was a bright day, I did my washing and hung my socks, pants and T-shirt across the bike to dry and proceeded to the breakfast room. Tucking into a full breakfast, a group who arrived last night came in and two of them sat at my table. They were from the lower 48 on a cycling holiday, travelling a set distance each day. Anyone struggling would be picked up by the transport on route, but they would all meet up again in the evening. One of the chaps told me he used to be a biker, but he married a lady who wasn't into bikes, so he had sold it - how sad. The driver of their transport appeared soon after - it was time for them to get moving. I noticed a few weren't walking very well, they must be finding it hard going. As I walked out from breakfast, I saw they were heading in the same direction as I was - Paxton. After I gathered my gear and packed my stuff sack, I checked the bike over. It was starting to lose a few of the bolts that were holding the fairing on and I soon replaced these with nylon ties.

The weather was nice and so I pushed on, enjoying my day. As soon as I arrived in Paxton, I blinked and was through it. Leaving the roadhouses behind, I saw my breakfast friends and gave them a wave. I headed on towards Delta Junction. The bike was running well and the scenery was great, so I stopped often to take more photos, even managing to take some whilst riding; surprisingly some of them came out very well!

Late in the afternoon, I drifted into Delta Junction where I headed to the café to have a sandwich and a pot of tea and also to plan the route for the evening and work out a possible stopover. There was a breakers yard next to the café and I wandered into the cold metal construction, thinking how cold it must be in the winter. There was a chap doing something to an enormous pickup truck. In my best English, which is difficult with the strong Cotswold's accent I have, I wished him a good evening and asked if he had any old Alaskan number plates. He directed me to a shack in the corner of the building and through the open door, I could see the boss slouched in his chair. When I explained my need, he struggled to his feet and, without another word, left through a side door. Amongst a load of old cars, he opened a door, reached in and produced a number plate.

On the bottom it read "the final frontier". It was just what I wanted - it's a boy thing! He handed it to me, refused any money and walked back to his shack. Thank you very much.

I was delighted with my number plate and I decided I needed to find the post office. Once there, the lady behind the counter helped me with the packaging and postage. There were T-shirts to buy with the Alaskan Highway on them and I proceeded to try one on, much to the amusement of the other customers. I bought one and slipped it into my package with my number plate and then off across the road to the shops for a few provisions and the essential fishing rod - boys will be boys! I found a small all-in-one kit and a gold pan, taped the reel to the rod and the rod to the back of my bike.

I left Delta Junction and was heading for Fairbanks when I saw my first moose only fifty yards away - what a big boy he was. He didn't seem to mind my being there and I took a few photos. There was also a calf grazing at the side of the road and I remembered reading that Mum would definitely be around somewhere, so I didn't hang around!

CHAPTER 9. "BAD NEWS" CAMP

As evening closed in, I started looking for a place to camp and tried a couple of tracks; one even had a cabin at the end of it. There was a small lake to my right, with a very flat area just to the one side, but, from my Milepost, I'd calculated that there must be a roadhouse about a mile farther up the road, so I decided to have a look before setting up camp, took the next track and couldn't believe my luck: there was the Midway roadhouse. I stopped for a cuppa and a chat with the owner. She was very pleasant and offered me a room for the night at a very reasonable price but, for some reason, I had liked the look of the campsite and decided to camp instead. That was the wrong decision, as I was to find out the next day. I thanked the lady, told her I'd be back in the morning and headed back to the camping area. There was plenty of wood about, so I soon had a good fire going. I went for a wander before settling down to eat and walking into the wood, I saw a cabin, then another and another. They were all empty and in disrepair, which seemed strange, but I found a nice piece of plywood to use as a shelter near the fire to warm the gear - and me. I fixed the plywood up as a roof, using a few branches and rope. This proved to be a good move, although it would have been even better with a canvas sheet. I soon had a roaring fire and settled down to eat and plan the next stage of my trip.

I was awoken the next morning by heavy rain. Whilst I lay there considering how to pack the kit without getting drowned, that roadhouse seemed very welcoming all of a sudden! Then all hell broke loose! I unzipped the door of the tent to find that I was being 'attacked'. Helicopter after helicopter were zooming over the trees, so low that I could see the whites of the pilots' eyes, but just as soon as they had come near, they were gone, no attack, thank the Lord. By this time it was throwing it down. The 'HQ ' was still standing so I decided to break camp in my shorts so that all I would end up with was wet pants. It all went very smoothly and soon I was drying out by the fire and warming up. After a last look around the now very wet camp, I fired up my bike, which looked extremely damp. The rain was still pouring and the roads were flooding. I could hardly see where I was going, so speed was limited.

When I spotted the roadhouse in the distance, it was a welcoming sight. I parked next to a BMW semi off-road bike, quite nice but very dirty - it obviously belonged to a traveller. Inside the roadhouse it was warm and cosy; I ordered eggs over easy, found a table and sat down with my large mug of steaming tea. On the next table was the traveller and I introduced myself. His name was Larry, a Yank from the lower 48, my first American pioneer. He had just ridden the Dalton Highway and I told him I remained undecided whether to risk this, having been warned about the heavy rigs (large lorries) and the number of accidents on that highway. Larry explained the drill: an approaching rig can be seen as a speck in the distance or a large cloud of dust. Once seen, he advised me to pull over and wait for the rig to pass. On passing, the drivers radio back to the other rigs to let them know bikers are on the road. That way, all parties are aware. Accepting Larry's advice, I decided I would ride the Dalton after all.

After an enormous breakfast, Larry announced he had to get moving as he had a long journey ahead. Just six thousand miles home to the lower 48, a true American adventurer. I watched him putting his gear on, just a pair of over-trousers, a leather jacket and an open faced helmet. This bloke was made of tough stuff, especially since it was still throwing it down with rain outside. As we said goodbye, he advised me to try "Yukon Jack" (a type of sweet whisky) and the Aron Motel in Fairbanks, as these are both cheap. After I assured him I would, he wished me all the best and was gone.

I settled into a conversation with a local chap, who seemed fascinated with my bike and trip. He wanted to know where I was heading and where I'd camped the previous night. He knew the place "Bad news, that area. About ten years ago, those living there became ill and all the vegetation started to die. Following a number of deaths, an enquiry found that the military had dumped toxic waste into the water course, polluting the water system and surrounding area. They never confirmed they caused the catastrophe and from what I could gather there was a big cover-up. The only way for people to survive was to move out of the area".

Well, that explained the widespread availability of dry wood and abandoned cabins. I noted there were no warning signs of any kind in the area.

Good job I didn't drink the water or wash in the lake!!

CHAPTER 10.   FAIRBANKS IN THE RAIN

Viewing the rain through the window, I reluctantly put on my gear.

The very wet bike fired up and was running remarkably well, considering the amount of water around.   Conditions were deteriorating, so the going was slow and I just couldn't see where I was going.   Nearing Fairbanks, I pulled under cover of a garage as I had decided to find the Aron Motel.   When asking the garage attendant for directions, I wondered why he smiled as he directed me.   It wasn't long before I found the Aron.

Hum …..very impressive?!   I could quite see why the garage attendant was smiling.   It consisted of a load of cabins, rather like the ones on container ships.   Despite appearances, I decided anything would be preferable to a tent today and stopped outside what I thought was the office. There was a man and lady inside and, when asking for a room, I got a story about how he'd spent some time in Europe and thought the women were a wonderful screw (his words). He went on to say how one tall leggy blonde was a particularly good screw and, as you can imagine, this boy did not impress me one little bit.   In fact, if it hadn't been raining so hard, I would have promptly disappeared.   Unfortunately, it was and so I followed him to a broken down portacabin with a leaking roof.   Well, it was better than a tent, but not much and there was no sign of a heater. The man told me they were extra - but he hadn't got any anyway! Great, a steel shed with no heater in the middle of Alaska.   I wasn't even completely out of the rain as I had to empty the bucket in the middle of the room!

When I started to remove my wet gear, the zip of my coat disintegrated.   I had a choice of getting a new zip or freezing.   Changing into dry clothes, I noticed the rain was easing , so I decided to walk into the town for food and a relaxing afternoon.   It was quite a walk, but luckily there was a shop that would stitch a new zip for me.   I managed to hail a taxi to return to the 'luxurious apartments' to pick up the coat and arrived back at the shop just before closing, to be told it would be ready by 10.00 a.m. the following day. I got back into the taxi and headed to the centre of town, arranging for the taxi to pick me up later that evening. I found a western style café and sat by the window to watch the world go by, feeling a bit warmer. There seemed quite a few Indians in Fairbanks and I found them quite fascinating. There appeared to be two standards, the very poor and the working class. I think my waitress was Athabascan. She was quite a large lady, quite an advert for the food, so I decided to chance it and ordered. It was a nice meal and I enjoyed it.

I finished my meal and decided to do a little shopping and found a very nice Alaskan T-shirt, one to add to the collection! I was also fascinated by the number of gun shops and the things available to buy. So many knives, quite a sight. I wandered back to the bar and waited for the taxi which surprisingly arrived bang on time. Arriving back at my plush motel ,I noticed a gathering of blokes standing around, chatting and drinking. With slurred words, they invited me to join them for what I think was an after-work booze-up. I accepted a drink and joined the conversation. It seemed some of them worked and some didn't - interesting!

A Vietnam veteran with, from my observations, a big drink problem, was particularly interested in me His conversations revolved around women and guns and he insisted that I went to his cabin and look at his gun collection; he also had some more at a friend's house. It didn't sound like a collection, more an arsenal. The more he talked, the more I backed off. This prat indeed had a problem. When he asked me to have another drink, I declined, saying I wasn't a drinker and couldn't take too much. However, he followed me back to the room. After a short while he left, only to return with a sub-machine gun. Oh Lord, what next? I was made to view his pride and joy. After another disappearing act, he returned with more beer. Needing to get rid of him, I said all the usual things like "I have an early start, it's been a long day, need to rest my back". Nothing worked, so I tried lying back on my bed and pretending to drop off to sleep. After a while, he became a dull noise in the background. I think I must have fallen asleep as he wasn't there when I awoke the next morning!

The room was very cold and damp, so I needed to warm up. As nothing else at this placed worked, I didn't stand much chance with the showers. I grabbed my towel and legged it to the shower block. Meeting another chap coming out, he suggested trying number six as that was the only hot one. I took his advice and enjoyed the hot water. I dashed back to the room, got myself ready and loaded my bike as the rain had eased up. I wired in my already prepared BMW 12-volt plug directly to the battery of the KLR - this was for my heated waistcoat. It was quite a fiddle, as there wasn't much room to connect the wires; there seemed to be too many cables at the rear of the battery. However, I managed to squeeze it all back in and refitted the cover. It worked - great.

I set off to find breakfast at the café the taxi driver had recommended the previous night. I was glad to be able to warm up, as I was only wearing my plastic Johnny jacket; I really hoped my coat with its new zip would be ready. I tucked into a good breakfast and two large mugs of tea deciding the route for the day - ride from Fairbanks to Fox and then onto the Dalton Highway.

In the background, I noticed a very attractive lady wandering around the café, dressed in period costume. She looked very good in a red flowing dress. She wandered over to where I was sitting and stopped for a chat. Apparently, there was some sort of celebration happening in Fairbanks at the weekend and she invited me to join in. When I asked her if she would be good enough to sit on my bike for a photo, she agreed.

Breakfast over and feeling human again, I left the table. The lady beat me to the bike and was already sitting on it when I arrived. I suggested she didn't lean back as it could topple off the stand. She sat nice and still while I took some photos - she was great fun and chatted away happily. After thanking her, I fired up the big single, and set off to collect my coat and new zip. Thank goodness, it was ready but it cost me 55 dollars, expensive but great service. Trying it on, the zip turned out to be on the other side, the way the Yanks do it. Still, I was warm and cosy, so whichever way the zip went, I didn't care. So…I set off on the next leg of my journey, on to Fox.

CHAPTER 11. DALTON HIGHWAY - AND THE ARCTIC CIRCLE

On my way again, north to Fox. The morning was cold and damp, but with my new zip and heated waistcoat switched on, it was good riding. A few miles on, I rolled into Fox and found a garage for fuel. Whilst paying, I spotted an off-licence attached to the garage and I asked whether they sold Yukon Jack. Apparently they did, but despite standing in the shop I couldn't buy any until I crossed the threshold into the actual liquor store. Once I'd done that, I was able to buy a bottle. Strange, but as that's the law, that's that.

Armed with the bottle I left, heading once again north on the Elliott Highway. For the first part it was tarmacadam, then dirt. As I rode on, the day brightened and I settled into a steady rhythm. There was very little traffic and I began to push on hard, crossing many bridges and creeks with interesting names, such as the Chatanika and the Tatlina. I would just pull over, have a look and maybe take some pictures, then off again. I have never done much dirt riding and to be quite honest never really fancied it, but this I was enjoying. First it was dust and dirt and then it changed to mud. This appeared to be the pattern on all the dirt roads I encountered throughout my adventure.

On the lower area there were three roadhouses. Giving the first two a miss, I pulled in when I reached the third one. It was a log cabin with a brand new shiny Harley on the front veranda. I think that was why I stopped. The proprietor was Gus, a great chap. Now the Harley - that was his. He had owned a bike as a young man but, unfortunately, had had a very bad accident that brought his biking days to an abrupt end. However, as he recovered from his accident, his dream was to own a Harley so, one day, he had taken his pickup truck to Fairbanks, bought a brand new shining Harley and brought it home to place it on the veranda. He hadn't even ridden it but the boy's dream had come true! Gus was very interested in my trip and asked how far I were going. He told me that if I crossed the arctic circle, I should call in on the way back for my certificate to prove I made it

I had a bite to eat and was ready to go again. As I left, Gus gave me a large bag of sweets and told me to look out for an old lady walking towards the arctic circle. She had been riding a bike, but had experienced so many punctures on the road that she had given up on it and was walking the rest of the way. Her name was Amy and the sweets were for her to wish her all the best. Apparently, this was the final stage of a five thousand mile ride/walk. I would certainly look out for her.

The road was drying out so, settling into a rhythm, I pushed on while the KLR was, once again, talking to me. I turned onto the Dalton Highway. The scenery was breathtaking.

So this was the Dalton, over four hundred miles of gravel, winding through the arctic wilderness, the lifeline of the trans-Alaskan pipeline. Truckers, miners and indigenous residents working together against the elements to help each other co-exist, travelled more by caribou than by humans, the last great highway on earth (got that out of the Milepost!).

I had settled into this ride and was enjoying it so much that I crossed the **Arctic Circle** without even noticing! After consulting my map, I decided to slow down a little to enjoy the view and take more photos. My padded handle grips were working very well and the bike felt great. The road was completely straight and I could see a long hill in front. I picked up speed and, approaching the hill, the KLR gave me all it had got. Once I'd topped the hill, I pulled in to a large flat area, resembling a lay-by, to find a sign announcing "Gobblers Knob". I wondered whether it meant the same in America as it did in England and parked my very dirty bike under the sign to take some photos. The view was magnificent and deserved to be recorded on camera. It was a nice spot and I sat with my Milepost to read about the area and the places I had passed. I also studied the map, planning where I could camp that evening.

I eventually decided to push on to Coldfoot as there was fuel and a campsite nearby, maybe also a café . Coldfoot is the place where would-be gold prospectors would arrive. Apparently, sometimes, as winter was setting in, they would get cold feet and turn back, hence Coldfoot. There was so much to see along the route and I regularly pulled over to take more photos. I rolled into the last roadhouse before Dead Horse. Once again, another enormous place with a petrol pump, tyre garage and café, so I decided to eat there. It was remarkably pleasant and there were quite a few people eating. A chap on the next table seemed to be taking a great deal of interest in me. He smiled and introduced himself as a ranger, covering the area from Fairbanks to Dead Horse, including Prudhoe Bay. He was interested in my adventure and asked where I was heading. I told him about the trip so far and that I hoped to make it to Prudhoe Bay. In his view, Prudhoe consisted of an oil facility, end of story. He told me there was nothing there - you couldn't even ride to the sea and, in order to reach it, you had to ride across one hundred and fifty miles of mosquito infested tundra, which he assured me wasn't much fun. He advised me to go as far as the Brooks Range and then down onto the tundra, just to have a look. I would seriously consider his advice.

He told me he rarely saw bikers this far north. He had come across a chap a couple of weeks ago from Japan. He was walking to Dead Horse pulling a shopping trolley with his gear in, mad or what, a Japanese pioneer. Apparently, there was another biker on the road today, on a very small bike, who seemed to be heading north. He told me to look out for him.

I was intrigued as to what the ranger did all day - surely there was little crime up here?

Apparently I was wrong. Drug criminals on the run from the lower 48, find this a great place to stash their ill-gotten gains - and they don't give themselves up easily, they fight!

Oh shit, who would have thought that? I wondered how he managed on his own. He explained he radio's out and reinforcements soon arrive - it can develop into all-out gunfights. This isn't England! The closest I get to action at home occurs when the cat next door duffs up the ginger tom from the council houses just up the road. Then all hell breaks loose! The ranger told me about a great place to camp for the evening: take the road north, ride about ten miles and look for a track to the right. Follow this track into the hills and at the end of the track there is a plateau, great for camping. I assured him I would look out for it and he wished me all the best. As I walked towards my bike, I saw the ranger's pickup truck, a wonder to behold. It was a very large one, enormous. There were gun cases complete with guns everywhere, wow. There was also a quad bike in the back and there were aerials protruding from every part of the truck - what a set of kit!

My first priority was fuel. This had to be a real top-up job, as this was the last stop for fuel until Prudhoe. The same applied if I decided to head to the Atigun Pass; I would need to carry extra fuel so I borrowed a three gallon can from the tyre garage, filled it and then strapped it across the bike. I also had to do a little maintenance on the bike. Because of the dirt roads, I had had to use the engine as the brake, which caused vibrations, shaking bolts loose which were responsible for holding things like mudguards, number plate, fairing, etc. I replaced them with nylon ties, which actually seemed to be working very well. All done, it was time to look for a camp.

CHAPTER 12. "LOADS OF WOOD" CAMP

I decided to try and find the ranger's camp site. Leaving Coldfoot, I headed north and after about five miles spotted two bikers moving south. Well, this was a turn-up for the book. The ranger didn't tell me about these chaps. Drawing level, we stopped and parked our bikes. They both had BMW bikes. We chatted for quite a while and I found that they had been over the Brooks Range and were now heading for the lower 48. Time to be on my way I wished them well and moved north again and it wasn't long before I found the track, quite narrow and a tricky ride. Then, as the ranger had said, there was the plateau with a wonderful view. One felt one could just sit and look.... and look and look..... Strangely enough I could hear a dog barking. In my Milepost, I found I was looking across the valley and the river Koyukuk, to Wiseman, an old mining town. Wiseman had come about in 1910 after gold seekers abandoned Coldfoot. Today there are about 25 residents, their number increases in the summer with the arrival of miners - the area remains a great mining area.

I set up my camp then needed to look for wood, none in evidence for a while then I was lucky, there was a great pile of wood. The good Lord must have seen me coming and dropped a pile of firewood just for me! So I christened this place "Loads of Wood Camp"!

The evening was beautiful, so with a good fire going and the meal cooked, I was able to sit and try to take in the wonderful scenery. I noticed I could see the highway - now and again a great dust storm would appear and thunder past, another rig racing to Fairbanks. I had gathered a large pile of firewood and fuelled a roaring fire. As the temperature dropped, it was a pleasure to sit by it, keeping warm and sampling the Yukon Jack. As the day moved towards twilight, I finally fell into bed at Lord knows what time, leaving the remains of dinner and the bottle where it fell. How stupid.

CHAPTER 13. MOUNTAINS, MOSQUITOES, BEARS, MOOSE AND TUNDRA

The sun was well up when I finally crawled out of my sleeping hole. The fire was still smouldering so I threw a few pieces of wood on and soon had a roaring fire, with the kettle on. Looking around I realised how stupid I had been the night before. Thank God I had survived. The remains of the dinner were littered around the place and the cooking and the smell of food could have brought the bears into the camp. Another lesson learned! I vowed I wouldn't leave things like that again.

Since I had been told that singing whilst having a wash was one way to keep the bears at bay, I wandered down to a small waterfall. I was just drying myself off, singing at the top of my voice, when I heard what seemed like a plane approaching. It was in fact a police helicopter, which came in really close. The pilot was waving to me, so I stopped my ablutions and waved my t-shirt, hoping he wasn't taking pictures. He seemed to hang around for some time but finally, with a wave, he flew on.

I decided to go back to Coldfoot for breakfast and find some hot water for a shave. In no time I was parking my bike - I think the thought of breakfast made the bike run a little faster! It was wonderful to have hot water after the cold stream this morning, but it had certainly woken me up. Feeling greatly refreshed, but with a slight headache, I tucked into a very fine breakfast, eggs over easy as usual, with a large mug of tea. My headache left me during the morning - I believe it was caused by Yukon Jack, not a very nice fella!

I decided to move north again and visit Wiseman, although I did want to get to Deadhorse by the end of the day. I soon arrived in a very small community of some ten houses. At one time, it was a very busy mining town. The houses were log cabins, some very nicely kept, others falling into disrepair. Wandering around I came across a chap building some sort of large shed. We had a little chat and I enquired whether anyone sold drinks. I was told to go and see Bernie in the next house, who had a holiday let... He appeared and welcomed me into his cabin where he lived with his wife and two month old baby. I think they must be very brave to have children in such a remote place.

Bernie worked for the government in the summer (forestry) and in winter he was a trapper. His wife ran a little gift shop. The cabin was cosy and warm but to spend the long winter here would not be for me. Some years before, I spent a very enjoyable Christmas with my daughter in Iceland but I didn't like the constant darkness, I asked how people managed and Bernie told me that some people do move south for the winter but, generally, people do last through the winter but, come spring, they shoot themselves. Shit - that's a bit drastic!

It was time to move on but I considered it was too late to start moving north - it would mean camping before Deadhorse again. So, I fired up the big single and was away - the track was very dry and dusty. As I approached the river, I dived into a right hander, lost the back-end and headed fast for the river. Deciding to put it down, I slid along the ground with the bike and ended up on the riverbank with the front wheel hanging in the river - a bit too close for comfort. Luckily, no harm was done to the bike or me! I moved on, heading for the Atigun Pass, following the pipeline and the River Dietrich. The weather was holding so this enabled me to push on, past Dietrich camp and onto the Brooks Range. As I started to climb, the weather closed in. It became cold and then started to rain so I switched my lifesaver waistcoat on to keep myself warm. I arrived at a very steep and slippery hill; it seemed I was riding on wet pebbles. The bike was jumping around and, at one time, it was difficult to keep traction. About halfway up, I passed a RV pulled into a lay-by. I did get a wave but was unable to return the gesture as I was fighting with the bike to keep it in a straight line and the shiny side up. Further on, I passed a car. At a quick glance, I spotted three women, who again were waving as I struggled past them.

By the time I finally topped the hill, I was riding on ice and it was snowing hard. The terrain seemed to level out and I was travelling between the tops of the mountains, quite high: the Pass is 4800ft above sea level and cold. Passing pump station 4, I entered Atigun Canyon, where I spotted some mountain goats. Hoping they had warm coats, I stopped and managed to get a few photos before the rain filled my camera.

Descending into the valley, the weather started to improve and it warmed up slightly. Running onto the tundra, with thousands of mosquitoes for company, I pushed on until I could see a camping ground. There were a couple of RVs and that was about it. If I was to make it to Deadhorse, I would have to just keep riding.

Eventually, because I was beginning to get tired, I decided to turn back, ride until the weather cleared and then find a place to camp. I pushed on through rain, ice, snow and cold. As I got farther south, the track began to dry out and I was able to slow down and take in Alaska in the twilight hours. Along a piece of elevated road, there were some lakes to my left. I stopped, with the engine running (a ranger had told me that if you stop on an isolated road you have to make some sort of noise to keep away the bears) and I witnessed a wonderful sight. A moose and calf were grazing in the lake, quite a sight to behold. They seemed unperturbed by my presence and, totally mesmerised by this wonderful sight, I was in a world of my own. I took some photos and prayed they would come out. The shutter jammed again but, with a little fiddling, it opened. After a while, the two wandered behind some trees and disappeared.

I pushed on and decided to aim for "Loads of Wood Camp" again I made it and it didn't take long to get the tent up, the fire going and the pot on. My dinner consisted of barbecued chicken and corned beef sandwiches, mustard, mayonnaise and bananas. I was really living it up! To top it off, I shared a joke with Yukon Jack, although that boy always gets his own back the next day. I sat and just tried to absorb the wonderful day, the great ride and this view again across to Wiseman. I decided I wouldn't go to Deadhorse after all, as I really didn't just want to see an oil facility. There was a great deal more to see in Alaska and this would mean moving south. I decided to sleep, but for some reason I was very edgy about the bears, this being bear country after all. After stowing the food and drink well away from the camp, I finally rolled into bed about 2.00a.m., shattered but happy. I slept really well, thanks to good old Yukon Jack.

The next morning I struggled from the tent and, looking at my bike, I immediately noticed a bolt missing from the rear suspension. Fortunately, the one on the other side was still in place. This was no nylon tie job, these were very important bolts. If I had also lost the second bolt, the back end of the bike would have parted company. After loading up, I put more wood on the fire until it was blazing - not sure why but probably because it was a good camp and I wanted to prolong it!

Sadly I rode away, taking it very steady, to Coldfoot for yet another breakfast - and the tyre garage. A young chap by the name of Deacon explained that he mostly dealt with tyres but he thought they might have some bolts somewhere. After about half an hour searching, he managed to find one with the right thread. It was too long, but I told him that it would be fine - I could manage - which I did with a bit of hard work. I did a little more general maintenance and was ready for off again - and breakfast.

During breakfast, I got talking to a chap called Ernie who worked on the pipeline and pumping stations. He was at the café to pick up his girlfriend, the café manageress. The Harley he had on his shirt started up our conversation. He strongly recommended me to stop at the old roadhouse at Finger rock "just say Ernie sent you" and I assured him I would call. Feeling very comfortable, I wandered out of the café and who should I bump into but the helicopter policeman! Apparently he had been looking out for me since that morning. "I saw you camped in the mountains the other morning and well, my boy, just a little way along from you was a grizzly and her cub, so I was keeping an eye on her for you" Thank the Lord for that! "Also, I followed you and in fact I clocked you at 75 mph on dirt, heading north!". "Who, me?" He smiled and told me to take it easy as he wouldn't be able to look after me today. He was heading straight back to Fairbanks after breakfast. Phew, that was lucky - seemed like a nice man though.

It was time to head off, so I fired up the big single and away I went.

CHAPTER 14. MOVING SOUTH

I hadn't been going long when it started raining, so I plugged in my suit and settled down to the ride. As I moved south, I started to run into heavy traffic - at least 2 cars and a rig, busy or what! On a long downhill straight, I noticed someone walking - wow, it was Amy, the walking lady! I turned and went back to have a little chat and to give her the sweets from Gus. She was delighted and told me to wish him all the best. She said she wasn't far from the arctic circle now - what a game lass!

As I headed off down the road, I spotted some bikers and stopped to talk to them. They were all from Mexico and had ridden all the way. Well, that is some way. They wanted to move on, so it was goodbye and I also pushed on to Finger Rock and Ernie's hot spot. The track to the roadhouse was extremely greasy and I was fighting to keep the shiny side up. At one point, I was going completely sideways, but I finally made it in one piece, parked my bike and wandered in. Immediately three ladies shouted out that they had been seeing me over the past few days. "We saw you in the Brooks Range and Atigun Pass". They commented on how cold I must have been, until I told them about my heated jacket. After tea, I wandered into the little gift shop, where I found yet another nice sweatshirt ! Wishing everyone well, I left - I had to find a post office to get rid of some of my gear and also to find some fuel, as I was running very low. There was a garage near Ray River. It seemed a little strange; the people who ran it appeared to be part of some religious group and seemed a bit odd. The fuel was expensive, but I needed it, so I paid up.

Pushing on again, I passed pump station 6 to cross the Yukon River to join the Elliot.

At mile 47, I was back with Gus and his Trading Post. "Did you make it to the Arctic Circle?" I told him I got as far as the Brooks Range and onto the tundra, some achievement. With a grin, he told me I looked a different colour to when I had left. I appeared to blend in well with the muddy track, real camouflage; it must have been quite hard for my helicopter policeman to spot me! Gus sold me a sweatshirt and two t-shirts and did my certificate - I had crossed the Arctic Circle, wow! He was delighted I had seen Amy and given her his gift. Again, it was soon time to move on. Gus had been so very nice to me, so I wished him all the best and I told him I would return.

Next stop was Fairbanks. I settled into a very wet ride and, after some way, I stopped at Midway Lodge which looked like any modern type building I was used to at home, not like the log cabins that I had grown accustomed to. I parked and went in, found a table and, as always, I took my coat off. The couple at the next table were interested in my back protector and asked what it was. I explained that it was basically padding to protect me if I came off the bike and they asked if I'd had to use it yet. "Only a few days ago, at Wiseman". I explained what had happened, their children were fascinated. They said it looked like a tortoise and I suppose you could say that. I had a meal and must say it was very average, as was the building. It was time to move again, so I wished the interested family goodbye.

As I started moving towards Fairbanks, the weather was clearing. I made the decision not to stay at the 'wonderful' motel, as I thought the tent looked more welcoming, as did a shower and a good night's sleep! There was a campsite full of RVs - impressive. One had to pay some sort of deposit at a machine, which I did in a fashion, with as few dollars as possible. I set about erecting the tent when I found out there were no showers - great, me stinking like a skunk, but I would have to make do until the morning.

I decided the site only catered for modern day RV adventurers - mobile mansions, complete with numerous showers. In fact, the one parked next to me appeared to be full of frightened people who never once appeared whilst I was there. Perhaps it was the smell! Anyway, I made myself something to eat then, feeling weary, I turned in. What I hadn't realised was that I had camped under the flight path for the airport, so every so often I was woken by a plane taking off. I definitely had to move tomorrow!

Hauling myself from my sleeping bag after a disturbed night, I crawled out of the tent to a very bright morning. Whilst I was waiting for the kettle to boil on my small gas stove, I gave the bike the once over. There was a couple walking in the road nearby and, in an instance, the wife was dispatched to wherever she had come from. The bloke slowly and nervously walked over to where I was standing and I wished him a hearty good morning. The conversation rapidly deteriorated from that point. "We don't hold with that sort of thing," he said. "What sort of thing?" I said. " You dressed like that". Granted, I didn't have any trousers on, but I was still decent in my underpants and t-shirt. I glanced down to check all was safely tucked away! It transpired that being stood in one's underpants and t-shirt just wasn't cricket, but it wasn't bothering me. Anyway, the gent in question decided I wasn't going to jump on his wife after all and he waved her over from her hiding place. He gave her the OK and she chatted away with me. Well, how very strange. After all this was America, the capital of the world, AIDS and any other sexually transmitted disease. You name it, they have it, and he was worried about my knickers. Prick! Finally, after a long chat they left. Although I had put my best conversation voice on - pure mid-England - hoping they would invite me for breakfast, there was no such luck! Anyway, I would most likely have had to put my trousers on!

I got my gear on and attempted to start my bike that had been overheating. The radiator was caked up with mud and it wouldn't start. I fiddled around with it, finally give the battery case cover a bang which seemed to do the trick. The entire panel lights came up and it fired up. The bright morning had now turned cold and very wet, in fact it started throwing it down. I eventually found a car wash and dropped a coin into the meter controlling the power washer. It was so demanding that I had to put about 8 dollars into it! However, it got the radiator clean and looking shiny again. My next concern was whether it would start again after so much water. Fingers crossed, it fired up. Next stop food, PLUS A SHOWER! There was a café with a laundry next door where I could have a shower - after the usual breakfast, eggs over easy and mountains of it! The waitress didn't hang around for long - she must have picked up the odour of skunks!

Well topped up for a while, I went to the laundry and, after depositing my washing into a machine, I got myself a towel and stood in line for a shower. The men were just in their trousers and the chap I stood next to looked as though he badly needed a wash - in fact he looked as if he had been half eaten. He relayed his fascinating story to me: a small plane had dropped him at a lake in the wilds. With a small inflatable boat, he had then travelled along various rivers and lakes, carrying only a few supplies. He had been drifting down one side of the river when, on the other side, he had seen bears. It must have been great fun. Finally, he found a floatplane and got a lift back to Fairbanks - at last a true American adventurer. Seconds later, he blew it totally when he asked me if I was Australian! I told him I was English, only to find so was he. My first true American adventurer had become another English one. He told me he had a gun and would never go anywhere without it. Looking at his lacerations, I asked whether he had been attacked. It turned out he'd arrived back at his cabin three days ago to find the roof was leaking. He had climbed a ladder onto the roof as far as the chimney, then slipped and fallen off. What a story - he had had a wonderful trip, survived, returned home only to fall off the roof. Can you believe it! Little did I know I was soon to find out how suddenly life can change. At least the good Lord had been with him until he returned home.

It was finally my turn for the shower and, armed with towel and soap, I proceeded to block the drains! It was wonderful, hot running water, one of society's luxuries. Shining like a new pin I reappeared and headed back to the RV park with my clean washing. At a hardware shop en route I asked for a canvas sheet. Despite seeing them in the corner I was told they didn't sell them. "If you don't sell them, then what's that?" "Oh, that's a tarp"! So I bought a 'tarp'(aulin)!!

My next stop was with the most northern BMW Dealer. George was a great chap, but far too busy to look at my temperamental electrics. Well, it was a Kawasaki, not a BMW. The dealership was his home - there was junk and old bikes everywhere. It was a must to get a sly photo or two which I had to show my local BMW dealer at home. He would never believe this - George is the most northern BMW dealer.

Back at the camp I took the tent down, packed it and loaded my bike. All jobs done, I decided to head out of Fairbanks on the Alaska Highway, towards Delta Junction. . The riding seemed easy, as I was back on tarmacadum, but I wasn't too happy about the amount of traffic I was encountering, like six vehicles in the last ten miles! My bike was OK - the radiator must have been the problem as it was now running very cool. I pulled in at a roadhouse, just north of wet camp. Following a welcome mug of tea I set off, aiming to reach Tok by afternoon.

Not far out of Delta Junction, I turned onto the Alaska Highway, which stretches in a north-westerly direction from mile 0 at Dawson Creek BC, through Yukon Territory to mile 1520 at Fairbanks, Alaska. Now heading towards Tok, I had been warned this road was very monotonous, just road and trees. That seemed about right. My first intention when planning the trip to Alaska was to ride the complete length of it but, after chatting to Tom, the bike hire man, on the phone he had convinced me there was a great deal more to see than road and trees.

I made the decision to start in Anchorage. Tom was right.

CHAPTER 15. "NO MOOSE CAMP"

As evening closed in, I started looking for a place to camp. I rode up several little tracks before finding a suitable place. Again, it was elevated but no river. I was really quite pleased with the sites I had found so far, but I certainly preferred those by the river.

I pitched the tent and then set about building the shelter with my new 'tarp'. I needed some long branches and found some which appeared to be birch or something similar - it looked like they had been cut down to create a clearing. It didn't take long to make a shelter (I would say the best shelter so far).

The rain had finally stopped and it was quite a pleasant evening. I got the fire going and the kettle on for the tea, but I was a bit short of water so I grabbed the kettle, put my helmet on and fired up the bike. I went down the track to the highway, turned north and soon found the RVs I had passed on the way in (today I would tolerate them!). I rode up to one with its door open (that was a first) to find some very scared human beings. They backed off as I walked towards the door. I gave a hearty good evening in my best polite English and asked whether they had any water to spare (of course they have water, they must have a tank full). Slowly they moved forward to ask how much I wanted. Producing the kettle, I waved it at them. Once they realised I was English, it was like a floodgate opening. They both went into raptures about how much they loved the English. Within ten minutes I had heard their life history. I was told all about their family and where they came from. Finally, with a full kettle of water AND a pot of jam (and a welcome to their home in the lower 48 any time) I was on my way. They were very nice and I wished them the very best.

Back at the campsite whilst my dinner was heating up, I wandered around the area and then saw that there were moose tracks everywhere. Panic! After a few thoughts, in my wisdom, I decided I'd be safe, as the camp I had made was on open ground. My theory was that moose preferred to stay in the woods (what did I know?!). I decided to stay put and sat under the new shelter, tucked into my meal, some tea and a little Yukon Jack. Whilst I was sitting there, a pickup truck appeared and stopped about 50 yards away. The chap looked a bit undesirable to me. Shortly after, he drifted off. I felt a little like the RV people - this unwelcome guest had unnerved me a little. I didn't like the way he just sat and looked at me. If he had spoken, I may have felt differently.

I made up the fire and crawled into bed - I think the Yukon Jack knocks you out as I had sweet dreams and slept like a log.

I crawled out to a dry morning and soon had the fire going and the pot on. I was running a little low on food so I decided to pack up camp and make for the nearest roadhouse. I was also in need of a wash. I took a few photos of the camp before packing the gear. Once my bike was loaded, I was ready to go. This camp had turned out to be a good, comfortable camp. I had managed to go the night without being eaten by bears, run down by moose or bothered by last evening's visitor. Fire burning, I left "No moose camp".

CHAPTER 16. "TOP OF THE WORLD HIGHWAY" TO THE CANADIAN BORDER.

After leaving "No Moose Camp" I rejoined the Alaska Highway. Again the road was straight with many trees and a little monotonous after the Dalton Highway. In fact, to ride the complete highway would be extremely boring; despite this, I would still like to ride the length of the Alaska Highway one day.

In no time, I found a roadhouse (lucky) run by two very nice ladies. I completed my ablutions and made my way back to the café and ordered a large breakfast (the usual, eggs over easy). I bought some postcards and sat writing these whilst waiting for my breakfast - my family must have been wondering by now what I was up to this time. I hoped my sons and daughter were finding the cards interesting .

All sorted, I decided to get moving. I thanked the lovely ladies and fired up my trusty steed and was soon burning up the miles to the next stop, Tok, which is located between the Tanana River to the north and the Alaska Range to the southwest. It wasn't long before I was rolling into Tok It seemed very small, mostly set on each side of the highway. I pulled in at the garage and fuelled up. There was a café nearby where I parked my bike amongst several Harleys (more bikers to chat to). However, the owners of the bikes turned out not to be so friendly, in fact they didn't even acknowledge me. Well maybe that was what the RV people were used to; it explained their reactions to me. I had read about the cult thing in America, but had really never taken it in. It transpired that Harley riders have very strong principles; one appeared to be "don't speak to anyone who doesn't ride a Harley" - obviously not true bikers. I did plug into their conversation though - they were moaning that if they took the "Top of the World Highway", they may get their bikes dirty or even fall off (what American adventurers)!

I made a quick exit and was soon on my way. I rode to Tetlin junction to turn onto the Taylor Highway, also known as the "Top of the World Highway" . This highway would take me across the Canadian border , then crossing the Yukon River to Dawson. Settling into a rhythm, I enjoyed the ride - this was a great road with the most magnificent scenery. I soon lost the tarmacadam, the road turning to stones and dirt - rough dry riding, but very enjoyable. I made regular stops as there was so much to see and many photos to take.

I noticed in my mirror a pickup truck, the only vehicle I had seen. He seemed to be hanging onto me and was very close. So, as a boy would, I responded (I took up the challenge) and pulled away from him. I had the advantage as I was leaving a hell of a lot of dust in my wake - the quicker I went, the thicker the dust became. The riding became quicker, but he also responded. On the long straights he would reel me in and on the bends I would lose him (oh, the thrill of the chase!). The mist came down and I realised he would never pass me. Straights and bends, we raced on. This lasted for about ten miles and then he was gone. I pulled in, but no pickup appeared. What happened to him?

Once again I settled into a steady pace. I wondered why I had raced, how stupid, but what fun! Boys, eh!

The battle won, I rolled into Chicken, not the most attractive place, but quite functional. It consisted of a collection of huts: Chicken Mercantile Emporium, the liquor store, saloon and Chicken Creek cafe. Time for a tea and a pee stop and a little shopping (a bottle of Yukon Jack). I intended to cross the Canadian border later that evening so, once finished, I fuelled just outside Chicken and pushed on.

The road was something else. I passed old mining works, then I came upon a dredge. To describe it, I would say it was a boat - it looked as if it would dig out in front and then float or be propelled forward and then do the same again. I managed to get a close look and a few photos. Later that day, when looking at my Milepost, I found the same picture as I had taken! It turned out to be 'Jack Wade No. 1 gold dredge', one of the first bucket line dredges used in the area. It was initially installed at Butte Creek but eventually moved to Wade Creek, where it rests today. I spent some time wandering around the dredge - it was interesting.

As the weather was holding, I decided to move on, settling into a steady pace trying, at the same time, not to miss any of the scenery. I had made good time, the American and Canadian borders loomed up ahead. I slowed for the American border guard and he waved me through. The Canadian border was a different kettle of fish! A lady officer stepped out. She demanded my passport and asked whether I was carrying a gun. I told her "No" - she seemed happy with that and waved me on my way.

I moved off towards a darkening sky and a sudden drop in temperature. Within five miles I ran into a terrific hail storm. On went the heated jacket and the going was slow. The storm lasted about ten minutes then it warmed up and the roads began to dry. Soon after, I crossed from dirt roads to tarmacadam.

CHAPTER 17. ON TO DAWSON CITY, CANADA

I rode hard towards Dawson. It was a great road with great bends. I had the KLR singing to me. I became more convinced that the KLR was a good all-round bike. I dropped down towards the Yukon River, what an amazing sight, I couldn't believe I was really doing this. As I approached the river, I passed a few cars waiting for the ferry. A chap waved me forward, shouting he had just enough room for the bike. I rode directly onto the ferry and more of less straightaway, we set off. The ferry took about ten minutes to cross the Yukon River. As we neared the shore, the ferry lined up and ran into the gravel bank - it was quite a bump and had I not been sat holding my bike, then it would surely have fallen over. The ramp was dropped and off I went.

All in one day: the Taylor highway, Chicken, the Yukon River, Dawson and the wonderful wilderness. Just fantastic. Gloucester boy on tour!

I was riding into town when I noticed piles of soil and rock everywhere. The prospectors had dug up every available bit of ground they could - there was nothing left unturned. As I rolled into town, it seemed life had not moved on, there had been very little change. The boardwalks and buildings were just as they had always been. Dawson is a frontier town with just a few prospectors and only a few cowboys left now. I found a food shop, parked up, locked my bike and wandered in. I needed water and food - they had everything. After a nose around, I came out with all I needed and loaded my bike.

I walked around a couple of streets. I kept expecting cowboys to appear from the saloon or around the next corner! I decided to have a good look around tomorrow - now it was time to find a camp for the night. I fired up the bike and very slowly drifted out of town, eyes everywhere. As I left, there were more heaps of rubble I could just imagine what it was like, how they survived the winter I didn't now. From what I had been reading, a great many died from the severe cold.

CHAPTER 18. "BEAVER CAMP"

About 4 miles out of town, I found a great camping spot, complete with small lake. I parked up and piled into my jobs. Quickly done, I set off to go fishing and spent the whole evening doing so, only stopping for something to eat. I caught numerous small fish which, for me, was great as I am not the world's best fisherman.

It was a pleasant evening and I was enjoying my first Alaskan fishing experience. All was quiet then, suddenly, there was a very large splash, rather like someone had dropped a very large stone into the water. This rather unnerved me as I suspected I was not alone.

After a good look around I found no evidence of other human beings. I settled down to my fishing. After a while, there was another big splash. Quite startled, I watched the ripples settle, then a beaver surfaced. He slapped the water with his tail. What a sight!

He swam around the lake and seemed not the slightest bit concerned by my presence. I was able to take many photos. I was fascinated by his antics. Unfortunately he disappeared as quickly as he had arrived.

I later found his lodge - a very large pile of wood. This was yet another highlight of my adventure, as well as the fact that I had also managed to catch six small fish, the first ones of the holiday!

After a nice evening, I turned in. I was pleased with this camp. First fish, then beaver. "Beaver Camp" was special.

CHAPTER 19. THE SPELL OF THE YUKON

The next morning was dry so I broke camp and headed into Dawson. Each side of the road was so interesting, heaps of rubble everywhere, every inch of the area had been dug up in peoples' search for gold. I arrived at Dawson to find a great café called Klondike Kate's - I think it was originally a saloon. After ordering, I settled down to a relaxing cuppa and the local information sheet. Breakfast was very good. The place seemed to fill up whilst I sat there - there was a buzz of conversation, you could just breathe in the atmosphere. Looking across the street I could see a poem painted on the wall of the building opposite. It read:

The spell of the Yukon
I wanted the gold and I sought it
I scrabbled and mucked like a slave
Was it famine and scurvy - I fought it
I hurled my youth to the grave.
I wanted the gold and I got it
Came out with a fortune last fall
Yet somehow life's not what I thought it
And somehow the gold isn't all.

It made me think. It was right at the time, but the years change one's view on life and one's priorities.

After devouring the wonderful breakfast, I left. I found the post office and sent more cards. I then walked around the town testing the boardwalks - it really seemed little had changed over the years. The whorehouse was still standing, but not in use. The original post office was open for special edition stamps, again a super building. I found the hardware shop, it had everything a gold prospector could ever need, it was a den. I fancied becoming a gold prospector so that I could purchase some of the wonderful gear, or a miner, a trapper. Oh - anything!!!

By the time I had finished browsing it was well past midday. I called back at the breakfast stop and had a little light lunch. The weather was still holding, so I decided to do a bit of the Dempster Highway. I didn't have time to do the complete trip to Inuvik, but decided to go as far as the Blackstone Mountains. I had been told that this was one of the most beautiful parts of the Yukon. I wondered how it could be any more beautiful than what I had already seen. I decided to do thirty miles to the Dempster and fifty miles up the highway. Fired up, I was soon tramping hard out of Dawson. The sun was shining and, once again, I was enjoying my riding.

The first thirty miles was on tarmacadam, but once I came upon the sign for the Dempster Highway, it turned to a dirt road. As I had been told, the route was magnificent. To my delight, I saw a couple of bald eagles soaring in the sky. I used my bargain binoculars to watch them for ages. Finally, I moved on, but very reluctantly. How many times in my life had I watched soaring bald eagles? A little farther on, I was watching arctic foxes playing in the sun. This truly was something else. I was alone in the Yukon, rolling hills, beautiful woodland and just so silent, apart from the roar of my bike.

The dirt road was muddy and very slippery in places. I think there must have been a great deal of rain over the last few days. It was very difficult to keep traction. As I reached the fifty-mile marker, I was finding it hard to keep the shiny side up. Time to turn back, I headed down the track for about five miles. It looked to me like gold country (dreamer) so I stopped and parked up. I got my new gold pan off the bike and did a little panning!

This was the first time I had used the pan I had purchased in Delta Junction.. As I was in bear country, I thought it best to sing at the top of my voice. I found no gold, only a dry throat! With no gold, I packed my pan and set off back towards Dawson. I would have loved to ride the Dempster Highway - this place was so vast it would take a lifetime and you would still never see it all.

The weather was still holding as I drifted into Dawson. I found a small café near the shore of the Yukon river and sat outside with tea and chips. I struck up a conversation with a Japanese couple. The chap was fascinated with my bike and the way it was loaded. He was interested to know about the adventure I was on. His girlfriend looked young enough to be his daughter. However, she seemed very happy and was obviously enjoying their travels. They turned out to be true Japanese adventurers. They told me they had just arrived in Dawson, having canoed six hundred miles down the Yukon river. Wow, how wonderful! They had stopped at Dawson to pick up supplies and have a cuppa. They had another two hundred miles to go and then they planned to sell the canoe, or give it away. After resting for a few days they would proceed with their trip around the world - not far then! They seemed very happy. We swapped stories and it was great. Soon it was time to move - who invented this time thing? I had to move on to the ferry if I was going to make the US border by evening.

My leg over my bike I once again fired it up and made for the ferry. I parked in line and had to wait this time as they were taking a tanker across and no other vehicle was allowed to travel with the tanker. Whilst waiting, I noticed another biker who wandered over to chat to me. His name was Steve, another American adventurer - gosh I had now met 5 or 6 American adventurers. From our conversation I got the impression he was looking for company so I invited him to ride along with me. I planned to set up camp once we had crossed the US border. He agreed. He made his way back to his very large Honda, most certainly not an off roader, to wait for the ferry.

The ferry arrived back - I rode on and stayed seated on the bike. There were about twelve cars and two bikes. The ferry rumbled off the shore with me trying to hold the shiny side up. Ten minutes later we ploughed into the shore. We were away. The border closed at eight o'clock and we were cutting it fine.

Soon the big KLR was singing to me. The road was tarmacadam. The evening was clear and the visibility was good, enabling me to ride fast. The KLR buzzed along between eighty and ninety mph. I saw no other vehicle between Dawson and the US border. I hammered the KLR - it was talking to me. The thrill of the open road was amazing.

CHAPTER 20. FUN, SPILLS, THRILLS

As I approached the border post, I noticed there were bollards out across the road. A Canadian guard stood outside the hut on the Canadian side. I pulled up and asked her how long the US side had been closed - just! I moved cautiously forward towards the bollards. As I did so, the US guard appeared and I moved towards his hut. "Little late aren't you?". I explained why I was late and told him there was another rider behind me. He seemed very amiable, or maybe he just liked the English accent. "OK, come across, leave your bike there and give me a shout when he arrives". I parked up on the other side of the border as instructed. Once he had gone back into his hut, I crept back to the bollards and realigned them and then sat and waited.

Steve appeared but there was no stopping him - he came straight through, hitting the bollards everywhere. At that, the border guard appeared. Steve, being a US citizen, had no problems with the guard. In fact, the guard wished us well and advised us to get out of the hills before finding a camp. Good advice as the cloud had descended.

Once again, I was away and within half an hour I ran out of the cloud. I pulled in and waited for Steve. After a little chat I set off to find a camping place and soon found a great spot. I think it had been a mining area but had been levelled. It was nicely elevated with the river visible below. We set to work to make our camp - tents up, collecting firewood, shelter built, then we did some cooking and tea drinking - and a little Yukon Jack.

My new travelling companion was called Steve O'Malley, some sort of engineer. This trip was his three weeks' holiday. He was very well equipped - he carried everything imaginable on his bike. Every tool, rope, tape, just everything the biker/camper needs. How he rides such a big bike on dirt roads and stays upright was a miracle to me. He seemed a nice chap and we had quite a good laugh. I think he enjoyed his Yukon Jack!

After dinner, I had a little wander to see if I could find a good fishing place - finding nothing suitable I went back to camp. Steve was turning in for the night so after packing my rod, I crawled into my sleeping bag. Bear infested country? I slept like a baby - a lucky baby!

Steve was moving around quite early, I just lay there until I heard his tent poles clanking. When I crawled out he was completely packed and ready to go. After stoking up the fire and making a cup of tea, I dropped the tent and packed my bike - and dismantled the shelter. Steve decided to ride to McCarthy. The town of McCarthy is a beautiful area of glaciers and mountains. The Kennicott river flows by the east side and joins the Nazina river which flows into the Chitina river. I wasn't too keen on this idea as the road to McCarthy was again dirt. Having been very wet in that area in the last few days I didn't fancy dropping the bike again at this stage of my adventure, but I would stay with him on some dirt until the turn off at Chitina, then I would head for Valdez. He changed his mind and we stayed together.

Once again we were away - he went ahead. I had become accustomed to my slow starting, always taking my time to look around and slowly build up my speed as the morning moved on. On reflection, this was not new. As a lone traveller I had been this way for many years. It became more obvious as I was travelling with other riders.

The "Top of the World Highway" was, once again, wonderful and I was taking in its beauty when this enormous bird swooped across in front of me. I stopped to watch it duck and dive, finally coming to rest in a tree not far off the trace. Slowly I moved forward, stopped and found my binoculars. It turned out to be the largest owl I had ever seen. It moved around on its branch, did a little preening and took very little interest in my presence even though my engine was still running. Having observed the owl for a while I slowly moved forward. When I was almost level with it, it flew off and I watched it disappear into the distance. I moved on - my pace quickened as the road dried out - Steve must be some way ahead as I had spent so much time with my owl.

I came across a filling station, topped up with fuel and had a cuppa in the little café. I was chatting to a chap who was working a claim near

Chicken. He said they were doing very well. I asked him how he managed in the winter and he said he goes home. Well, it must come to a standstill in wintertime and then when spring arrives, they start up again.

I fired up the KLR and pushed on through Chicken heading the only way I could towards the Alaska Highway. About an hour later, I passed Steve, then totally focused I pushed on towards Tok.

Having enjoyed my Taylor Highway, I drifted into Tok. My first job was to fuel the bike and I did this at the same garage as before when I passed through a few days ago. This done, I went to the same café (pleasant surprise, no Harleys!). What a nice little café, without the Harleys! After ordering my tea, I had a little flirt with two nice ladies, who loved my accent (what accent?), oh, that Cotswold accent! It feels good to have a dialect. When I was younger, I disliked my accent but now I am happy with it. Just think I could have been normal (what's normal?!).

Steve appeared and came into tea. He had also fuelled-up, so after finishing our tea and discussing what route was next, we left Tok and pushed on towards the Copper river, taking the Tok cut off. This road was once again tarmacadam, good riding. In places the permafrost had torn the surface up. The process seemed then to be digging out that part of the road and filling it in with chippings, then when this had settled in, they would re-surface. I worked out the only way to keep the shiny side up when I spotted the chippings (this could be 2 yards or 20 yards), was to drop down a gear keeping the revs high and power across it fast. This was all quite tough riding so eventually when Steve caught up with me we decided to find an eating house, fuel and food to take with us for our next camp.

Slowly we motored on towards Gulkana where we found a very large garage, store and eating house - I say large, not just three shacks, but double shack size and modern. Here we fuelled, then went to the café and had a 'breakfast' in the afternoon. I took myself to the store. I had noticed Steve had a Leatherman type knife so I was looking out for one. They only had cheap ones but I bought one anyway as well as some fishing spinners, food and water.

Tank full, stomach full, bags full, we moved off towards Glennallen and motored on for about an hour until we came upon a garage - with yet another shop!. Great. They had the most wonderful spinners so, yes, I bought some more. I think this was in anticipation that I would catch a large fish - dream on! I chatted to the chap and asked if he knew a good camping spot - well yes and it was only a mile down the road. After taking directions, I thanked him and we were on our way.

CHAPTER 21. "SALMON FISHING CAMP"

About a mile up the road, I saw the track to my right. As I turned down, I saw some great camping places. . This looked a great area, quite large so we parked up while I looked for a suitable place.

I went towards the river (I wonder why?!) but after coming close to dropping my bike several times in deep ruts, I turned around and made my way back to find Steve waiting. So this time I set off to the right. The ground was quite flat and looked as if there had been a few campfires - looks interesting. I came to an area that looked fine but then noticed a large half-eaten animal carcass - shit, bear country. As I was busy looking around at all this, I hit a rock and fell off the bike (bollix). I was fully loaded and unable to pick the bike up. I looked around at the same time shouting at the top of my voice. Oh damn, calm down, think. Power, start the engine - it started and as I let the clutch in, it started going around in circles on the ground, with me running around with it. I pushed and shoved and finally it gripped and I stood it up Oh, thank God for that. I leapt on and away I went, not stopping to look around. I was sweating streams, so I headed back to Steve who was still patiently sat waiting.

I then went left and, there it was, the perfect camping area. I went back and got Steve and we started making camp, soon having the tents up and the fire going, cooked dinner and drank lots of tea. We sat around the fire and chatted about the day and our fishing tomorrow. I then turned in after another good day.

I slept very well and awoke to warmth, yes - the sun was shining as I crawled out of the tent. I gave the fire a poke and it was still smouldering and soon I had it going and the kettle on. I decided I was going fishing for the day and Steve said he was away to buy a rod and tackle, plus some spinners for me (what more?!) I set off through about one hundred yards of woodland to the Copper river, singing at the top of my voice as I walked along. Oh well, just look at this. The river was sweeping down into a long right hand bend, wide and beautiful. The river's edge varied so much - there were trees, steep rocks, pebble beaches. Oh Lord, no one is moving me from this river today - well maybe a bear would, ooooh.

I set up my little telescopic rod, fixed my best spinner, took my coat off and settled down, quite forgetting that I should be singing. The water was playing a great tune - who needs to sing? (brave of me). Within minutes, I was into my first fish. I battled for at least thirty seconds and landed it. What a monster, must be at least three inches long! By this time, I was totally fired up. I thought of my sons and what their remarks would be about my first fish of the day. They have always considered me not a very good fisherman, justifiably so. In fact they always say if Dad is catching fish they must be giving themselves up. Little did I know I was about to experience the best day's fishing I have ever had in my life.

The real excitement started within an hour. I was just casting out and reeling in when WHACK 'it' grabbed my spinner and took it down river (oh it's a whale). I hung on, slipping off the rock I was on and went straight into the river, complete with my motor cycle boots on. My motor cycle dealer at home will never believe I was just motorcycling with his best quality boots when I take them back demanding a new pair under guarantee!

Oh what the hell is on the end of my line? I scrambled out of the river trying desperately to calm myself down. Standing up I slowly let the line run, it was then I caught sight of the monster - it was very large, like two feet long, ooooh Lord! It's a silver salmon.

WOW, up it came, breaking the surface, it took a look at me, shook its head and was gone. Oooh bollix, lost it. This was the first large river fish I have ever hooked into. I was elated - but the toe rag had taken my spinner with him.

So I tied another spinner on and away I went again. BANG, ooooh another. Calmly I played him, trying to remember what my sons had taught me, after he had taken most of my line miles down river. Very slowly, I was reeling him in, confidence soaring. At last I am a fisherman. This one let me play him for a while, but when he had had enough he leapt out of the water, looked at me, shook his head and was gone. The pattern continued all morning. I was so engrossed in my fishing that I never saw Steve standing next to me. I gave him the lot. "Steve, I am on a salmon run, I have hooked dozens there, 4ft long and I am going to get supper!" He had ridden sixty miles to get his fishing tackle and also brought me food and a drink.

Hurriedly Steve got his tackle together. At that I hooked another - Steve couldn't believe it. As I played this one, Steve was advising me. He obviously was a fisherman as I got the fish very close to the shore before it came out of the water, looked at us and was gone - shit this happens all the time. Steve had a look at my line and said "you will never catch one on that, it's like cotton". At that moment, I hit another, ooooh Lord, hold him, hold him. I was doing my best and between us we got him right to the edge. Steve said he would get around behind him - he stepped into the water to get him and bang, he was off, spinner and all. Oooooh, lost another!

"Right", said Steve "we have to change your line", so he set about this, after casting his own line out. He said that I played them fine but couldn't imagine how I had done it with my line - "just skill, Steve"! Another "bollix" from Steve - damned yank.

"How many have you had on?". "about ten" I said, "well we have to land one now and we could have it for dinner". "I know, I know, that's what I was working on". "Where did you buy this rod?" he said. "It was a job lot - it came complete with the reel". "It's crap" said Steve - well that's nice!

We settled down to a little more fishing. We sat late into the evening, finally dragging ourselves away without a single fish. This was the 'one that got away' story, but thank you Lord for the best day's fishing I have ever had. Because we had had such a good day, we decided we would set off for Valdez , then maybe we could fish there tomorrow. I dropped the tent and soon loaded up and we moved off. Getting out of the place wasn't too easy - having got through the ford, it was flat out up to the top of the bank, then picking our way out between the boulders to reach the road. We turned towards Valdez.

CHAPTER 22. VALDEZ

We settled into a good pace and, as always, I was enjoying my riding. I covered a quick forty miles, at the same time looking for fuel and an evening meal. I then found a small complex with garage, shops and café, so I pulled in, got fuel, and parked up. I was off to the shop as usual - it took me a while to get around it - well, it's Alaskan, so I must look! The shopper - that's me!

Steve was with me as I left the shop and our next stop was the café where we ordered and settled down with two large mugs of tea and then some sort of pork with chips. It was very nice and I felt very comfortable as I left the café. My trusty steed was waiting; I untied her, fired her up and away. Next stop Valdez.

Valdez, located on Port Valdez.(pronounced Valdeez), an estuary off Valdez in the Prince William Sound. Valdez was established in 1897-98 as a port of entry for gold seekers bound for the Klondike goldfields. Thousands of stampeders arrived in Valdez to follow the all-American route to the eagle mining district in Alaska's interior and, from there, to the Yukon river and Dawson City and the Klondike. The Valdez trail was an especially deadly route, the first part leading over the Valdez glacier where the stampeders faced dangerous crevasses, snow blindness and exhaustion.

Valdez has moved. It was located about 4 miles east of its present position.. However, in 1964, the Good Friday earthquake hit south central Alaska, virtually destroying Valdez. The quake measured between 8.4 and 8.6 on the Richter scale. A series of waves centered in Prince William Sound travelled towards the land, causing massive landslides that swept over Valdez Wharf and engulfed the downtown area. After this, Valdez was re-located.

Construction of the Trans Alaskan pipeline began in 1977 and Valdez was chosen as the marine terminal. The site covers 1000 acres and the pipeline runs from Prudhoe Bay on the arctic ocean to Valdez. The 45 inch pipe runs for 800 miles.

The weather was holding, the road was good, the scenery was fantastic. As I approached the mountains I could see the glacier. There was a lot of pointing and shouting to Steve as I motored on slowly, although visibility was getting less and less and, finally, I had to pull over. I was just removing my helmet when Steve pulled up alongside me. My helmet was completed covered with dead mosquitoes so he immediately produced the visor spray, complete with cleaning rag, and soon had it clean and shining (what a boy!). Again, we pushed on, seeing very little traffic, but could now see in the distance, the lights of Valdez.

As we approached, I began to see buildings and people, the first town I had seen for a week. Bars with people, shops with people and roadhouses with people. We found the river and a RV park, quickly pitched our tents as it was starting to rain. I was in the tent and settling down for the night. This was to be the pattern of Valdez - unsettled weather.

After a good night's sleep, I was awoken by heavy rain. I broke camp quite early, my bike loaded, I was off into town, looking for breakfast and a place to have a wash and clean up. I found the sea front with lots of little shops and eating houses. "How would you like your eggs" "over easy" (!) In I went to Oscar's and tucked into a large breakfast for the princely sum of 3.95 dollars. Oh nice. Breakfast was a long job today, I was staying out of the rain. Even now I was looking at people whom I found very interesting. This was Valdez - interesting and fun. I did my ablutions in not the best of places, but it did the job.

After having another cup of tea, the weather decided to clear, so I took myself for a walk along the harbour, looking in this and that shop. This is a very interesting place, quite a few fishermen, travellers and a few Alaskans. I bought a few postcards and then went to find out about the canoeing trip I wanted to do the next day. I went into the office - the lady there was very helpful. She asked had I used a canoe before I said "yes, a little". She then said it was a two-seated canoe and I asked if there was another amateur who I could go with. "that's fine" she said "we can sort something out. I had to be down by nine o'clock in the morning. The lady said they would have to run through the safety procedures and a short lesson on canoeing first. That's fine.

I then drifted along the street, finding a fishing charter shop and. booked in for a trip in an hour's time with Steve. I wandered around looking at boats and people, all busying about, doing things. I had a drink and finally wandered to the boat. There were a few people waiting and then, after a short while, a lad appeared and said the captain would be along in five minutes. This seemed to create some confusion as to what the captain was doing - it turned out that one of the other boats had broken down and he was up to his ears in oil and dirt, trying to repair it.

Finally, after half an hour, the captain arrived, still a little oily. He had a quick wash in the fish bucket - he looked clean and smelt wonderful!! . Steve had also arrived and straightaway hit it off with the captain. Slowly we went down the harbour, picking up speed as we left - "should be a great day's fishing" said the skipper.

After running for half an hour, we were getting the rods set up, baited and out. This is the stuff. Two hours later we had caught nothing - there was also quite a swell running, so I wasn't feeling quite right. The skipper then said we will head for another area, we always catch some there. Ten minutes later, Angela the American lady hooked into a very nice silver. I was a little envious (understatement). Well, just look at the size of the thing. Green as I was from both angles, I then hooked into something big. Wow! As it broke the surface, I saw its shining silver outline and at the same time, felt the power of the fish as it dashed away. I walked around the boat, slowly hauling it in - the skipper was ready with the net - it was in the boat!! The first one I had landed, so to speak. It was large, about two feet long (this is not a fisherman's tale - well maybe just a little bit!). Well this looks like a good meal to me. Was I proud or not?!

My fish was the second fish of the day and the total catch numbered TWO!

My sick feeling had gone away whilst I was landing my fish but now the wind had picked up and it was raining quite hard. I was just hanging on in there when we entered the harbour (thank goodness). It was very bleak out there. I grabbed my salmon and legged it to my bike where I was sick (in private). Feeling better, I settled down to clean my fish, put it into a plastic bag and tied it to the rear carrier of my bike. I headed to the 'evening breakfast' stop, Oscar's. It was chucking it down as I pulled in and, over dinner, it was decided that we would find a motel for the night, no camping for me.

But what about my fish? Steve suggested that we buy some ice and pack it in that so he asked the lady at the café where we could get some. She told him where to go and he was off like a shot, returning with a special icebox and a large amount of ice. The fish safely packed and, once again, anchored to my bike, I put my wet weather riding gear on and plugged in my heated jacket and we went looking for a motel. After riding only a short distance, I found the Keystone Motel and was able to park right outside the door, being a little concerned about my fish! It was to spend the night tied to the carrier of my bike - what about the bears you may ask, or dogs, anything that was hungry? My thoughts were they wouldn't come out in the rain!!!

I paid at Reception and headed to the room. It was very nice, warm and cosy and a chance to warm up with a shower. I was tired, so to bed. I think the sea air and fishing takes it out of you. As I drifted off to sleep, I was thinking "I hope it's not pouring down in the morning for my canoeing trip........."

CHAPTER 23. THE CANOEING TRIP

I awoke to what seemed to be a bright morning, but I think we must have had a very wet night. I put as many thin layers on as possible, incl. my modern long Johns and then my Johnny jacket. Was I warm? I think so!

Steve had decided to start moving south. I will be sad to see him go, we got on very well. I had enjoyed his company very much. He was certainly not a first timer, I had great respect for him. I was ready to go but first I must find some food and a drink. There was a breakfast area situated on the landing at the top of the stairs - it was buns and tea and sort of snack things, which were fine. I also helped myself to various sashes - tea, powdered milk, sugar, coffee, herbal tea and anything else that was going! These things were a great asset when camping. I struck up a conversation with an Australian lady who, at a guess, was well into her eighties. She told me she was travelling Alaska on coaches and buses and was enjoying her holiday very much. Well, what a lass.

I packed my bike and set off for the Quay. I was early so I had half an hour to take another look around. I shopped a little more and posted a few things to my family. I also found a genuine native knife - I had been looking for one during all my shopping trips. I bought it - then thought how was I going to send it home - again!

Steve had also been shopping and appeared outside the café . This is goodbye. Sad. I thanked him for his company and also his fun - he fired up the 'big four' and was away. I am not a very goodbye person, in fact I am a baby. I quickly fired up the big single and was off, making my way to the boat yard. Already there were people milling around, waiting for the canoe people to arrive. The shop opened and we all filed in. I booked in. I also asked if they had a fridge where I could leave my salmon (which I had found this morning, still attached to my bike!). Yes, no problem, so I handed it over to the lady in charge. "Right, see Joe and he will kit you out. Life jacket, hard hat and Wellingtons ."

We all gathered outside the office. The leader for the day introduced himself. He was from the lower 48, but having said that, he seemed a nice chap! We all had to exchange names and places of origin. Our leader then asked "how many pairs have we", at the same time counting the group. He asked if we all had someone sorted out to canoe with. I had palled up with a chap when we were in the office, who said he was a "dickhead" so that suited me. That settled, we went through the short training lesson. This was interesting - we were told how to get into the canoe, how to get out of it onto land and also how to get out of it in the sea (that would be cold!). We then went on to the paddling instruction. The entire group was intent on listening - it was important

The instruction over, we made our way to the Quay. My new friend and I were allocated a canoe and we loaded it onto what looked like a beach landing craft. This done we waited for the others - I observed that one couple were in shorts - Lord that must be cold.

All the canoes were on and the captain boarded and we set off out of the harbour. This was a slow gentle ride, giving us plenty of time to look at the boats and the comings and goings in the harbour. Suddenly, as we left the harbour, he hit the throttle, the back of the boat went down, the front came up and away we went. Wow! We were flying up towards the glacier. The wind was very cold and most of us sat down in the boat - the lady in the shorts looked how I felt - cold. We travelled for about half an hour, now moving so fast I couldn't stand up to have a look about. Finally, we were slowing and heading for a grass-type beach area. The rain had stopped and it started to brighten up a little.

We unloaded the canoes and got them into the water. My new friend was chatting away, our boat in the water, I waded in, ready to get in, when I felt this wet sensation in my boot as it filled up with water - wonderful, I'd got a pair of Wellingtons with a hole in - damn! Well, I'll just have to live with it - at least I'm not in shorts. I was up front as James, my new friend, made it to the canoe. We were floating. It was quite amusing watching some of the party getting into their canoes, but good fun! I think they all realised that this trip would be great if everyone listened to our leader for the day.

With everyone in the water, we bunched together. Our instructor then gave us the route we would be taking. He also said not to spread ourselves out, keep sensibly close, we are a group. He could then come to anyone's assistance, if needed. I was, apart from my constantly wet foot, enjoying this very much.

We set off towards the glacier. I was glad to be as fit as I was because we had some way to go. The canoe seemed to glide through the water with ease - well, it's not really a canoe, it's a sea kayak. We headed towards the glacier and against the current. Our guide took us then to what looked like some small islands and a lake, also a rapid. He powered up the rapid, turned and came back to us - it looked so easy. Then it was our turn. We failed miserably so we had to beach the boats and walk with them. I squelched along until we found calm water; we got back into the kayak and moved off, now having to avoid a small ice flow. We pushed on against the current and could see the glacier in the distance. As we got nearer, the ice flow was getting larger - our instructor had said to keep well clear of them as 90% is below the water and they have a habit of rolling, which would take a small canoe straight under, so everyone was steering clear of them.

Someone spotted a bald eagle soaring above us, so there was a lot of photos being taken. It was just great to sit and watch his progress on the thermals above. We moved on, with our guide waving some stragglers in as we seemed to have lost our group. He was making for a beach area, pebbles and boulders, and we all managed to land safely. Our instructor told us to carry our boats some 100 yards up the beach. "Why?" I asked. He told us one previous group had 'beached' and then a large piece of ice had broken from the glacier and caused a large wave, this in turn washing their boats away. A boat had to be called to rescue them. So, after carrying the boat up the beach, we found a nice place to stop and have a drink and a bite to eat. Our guide had brought food for us all, but most people had brought sandwiches, so we had quite a feast! After lunch we carried our boats to the water and, once again, set off towards the glacier, at the same time seeing more wild life. I saw many seals - they surfaced and just looked at you, their heads seemed enormous. We also saw many different species of birds.

Once again, there were a few stragglers, as there was so much to see, so our guide gathered everybody up and we continued paddling towards the glacier. After about an hour, we were approaching the glacier so we beached our boats about 500 yards to the left of it and then carried the canoes a long way up the beach, when our guide said "did you hear that piece of ice hit the water?". He said you are about to have a demonstration of how boats could float away and it wasn't long before we saw the wave coming - it was quite an amazing sight and, it reached our canoes, just. I was so pleased to have witnessed this but also very pleased with where we had put our boats.

So, our boats in place, we started walking across the glacier, my foot getting colder and colder. We were on ice and there were a few crevasses. This is the sort of thing you read about and, look at me, I am doing it! It was quite hairy walking around these deep holes but the guide knew his way and led us quite close to the glacier face - I just hoped my camera was working as I was clicking away. As we progressed, the glacier was creaking - it was quite weird.

The cold was getting to everyone, especially the lady in shorts(!), so we made our way back to our boats. As we did so, the glacier seemed to be groaning, just as I was about my now, quite numb, foot! We arrived at the boats and got them into the water, grouped up and then with our guide leading, we headed towards the face of the glacier. We had strict instructions not to get too close to the face (I didn't need telling). It was a very slow paddle towards the glacier. There were lots of photos but, this part of our trip was quite frightening as pieces of ice were constantly falling off, at the same time pushing the larger ice flows towards us. The guide turned us away from the ice, towards the sea. This was all so wonderful - Cotswolds boy on tour!!

A good steady paddle soon took us south and away from the glacier. Again we saw a few more seals (how often have I seen seals in the wild?), plus the sight of two bald eagles soaring above us. How often have I seen bald eagles - I haven't - stop repeating yourself!!

Our guide started moving us on to our pickup point, about two miles away, so it was dig in and first back (a race!!). My new friend and I dug in hard, he seemed very fit, as I think I was. Over the last half mile, several canoes were level with us. We were both working hard and seemed not to be struggling and, very slowly, we moved ahead, reaching the pickup area some fifty yards in front of most of the them. We were both puffing a bit when we finished, but it was good fun!

The landing craft was waiting for us and after loading our boats, we got under way. It had been a great day and quite an adventure. Once again, we had a great and fast run back to the harbour. The poor lass in the shorts was in quite a bad way, so very very cold. I could see the relief on her face as we docked. After unloading the boats, we made our way to the shop and dumped the gear. I thanked them for a wonderful day, at the same time asking for my salmon from the fridge. I tied it to the bike and made a dash for Oscar's - nosh at last, plus warmth. I had just started into my tea when who should walk in but Steve. I looked at him and said "what's going on?". He said "I have had to work on the bike - oil leak. Still leaking a bit but should be OK" I said "did you have the right tools for the job?!" He cuffed me around the ear and, once again, we said our goodbyes. "Keep the shiny side up" - the big four roared away. So sad to see Steve go, he had been great .

The chap, James, whom I had shared a canoe with, wandered in. We chatted a bit - he was touring with his pal, not on a bike but in a great big four-wheeled thing. Their next leg was to Dawson. I wished them well and they were pleased with the directions I had given them. As the weather was brightening up, I decided to camp. A chap I had met a few days ago had recommended camping at Mineral Creek, so after a look at the map and feeling quite full and warm, I left.

CHAPTER 24. SALMON ON THE MENU AT MINERAL CREEK

I set off, it was nice to be riding again. I got onto a great dirt road - the wilderness once again. I kept seeing the river to my right but didn't seem to be able to get the bike to it somehow. I did find a couple of places but I had that feeling "don't camp there", don't ask me why. I was several miles into this road, enjoying every bit, when I came across this rather wide area to the left, with tree cover, so a great place to fix up the canvas sheet (the tarp!) Yes, ideal.

I parked my bike and soon had the tent up, bedroll and sleeping bag set up, all tasks completed. I went looking for firewood . The wood wasn't too plentiful - well, it was, but very wet. I arrived back at camp with my wood and then set about building my usual shelter with the tarp. I got a rope, tied it to the corners of the sheet, scrambled up the bank, pulled it around the trees and then pulled the sheet up. Job done. The shelter was about six feet off the ground and then, with a struggle, I got the fire going and detached the fish from the rear of my bike. Most of the wood I had collected was wet, so it took a little time to get the fire going. Once it was going, I placed the other wood around it to dry it out and then set about cooking my salmon, cooking it in some foil. I sat Yukon Jack-ing and tea-ing whilst the salmon simmered.

The evening was dry and pleasant. I kept the fire going and had now got a good supply of dry wood. I decided the salmon was ready - the foil was drawn back to reveal this beautifully cooked pink salmon. This was backwoods cooking at its best! I tucked into the fish, making very little impression on it whatsoever. The bit I had went down so well, complete with my assortment of condiments, and a little bread. I think by the time I fell into bed I had eaten about a third of this enormous salmon. It was very big - not a fisherman's tale!. I crawled into bed - stuffed!

It was a bright sunny morning as I emerged from my tent. I first checked the salmon out - yes, all in tact. I stirred the fire, it smouldered and I soon had a flame - on went the kettle! Then I opened the salmon and just had a taste - wonderful! I made the tea and settled to eating a little fish. There was plenty left for breakfast and lunch. Well, it was a good job there was enough because a walker appeared and stopped. We chatted; he drank my tea and ate my salmon!! He was very impressed with the flavour. He told me where he was heading, quite a nice walk by the sound of it and he said I could get quite a way on my bike, so I decided to give it a go. The walker then disappeared into the distance, full of my salmon!

Taking my time breaking 'salmon camp', I loaded the bike, finally setting off up the dirt road. I did about two miles then encountered a landslide and couldn't get past without probably falling about 60 feet to the river. I parked up and decided to have a walk. It was very hot but, having said that, it was a great place to walk, the river on the left, sometimes you could see it and then it would be gone, hidden by the trees. A steady walk, which took me all morning, before finally arriving back at my bike.

CHAPTER 25. BACK TO VALDEZ

After my morning's walk, I took a very slow ride to Valdez, stopping only to look for other camping places on my way. I found a great one near the river which I could use later, if I decided to camp. I arrived in Valdez and walked into Oscar's.(- what eating again?!)

I had now decided that tomorrow, I would leave, taking the ferry to Whittier and also to stay in a motel tonight, in case it rained. This would save packing up and getting wet if the weather had changed. Having polished off lunch, I made it back to the motel where I had stayed with Steve. I dumped my gear but my priority was to find a place and power wash my bike and do a little maintenance, plus get some fuel. I found a garage just down the road from the motel. This was great and I managed to do all the jobs.. The bike looked a lot brighter. I seemed to have lost more bolts, so nylon ties were taking their place, the complete fairing was now held together with ties. Fully fuelled I went back to the motel, parked my bike and re-loaded it. It was now ready for morning.

I had a shower and shave and looking and feeling better I decided to walk into town. On my way, I dropped into the motel laundry. The lady there told me that I couldn't use it until after 5 p.m. Fine, so I set off into town, first of all finding the Information Bureau. I wanted a native Alaskan shop, also the museum or some sort of place with information on the history of Valdez and the surrounding area. They directed me to a native shop just around the corner. The museum was just two streets away.

I walked into the shop and was greeted by an Alaskan lady. I asked about Alaskan knives - oh yes, she has a cabinet full - however, on inspection, I thought they were not truly native. The shop lady was very helpful and did say the knives were made in the lower 48. She explained that real original native knives were made of bone, not steel and said if I kept looking I would get one, but it would be steel as the native Alaskans now make them

from old files or whatever metal they can find. So, after a good look around the shop, I drifted on and found the museum. This turned out to be very interesting and there was a complete section on the Exxon Valdez oil tanker that ran aground some ten years ago. Terrible environmental damage has been created by this catastrophe. Apparently two thirds of the oil carried by the tanker was never recovered. A great many sea creatures and fish have been badly affected and the environment will be affected for many years to come, some things and creatures will never recover. There was also a section on a cruise ship that had run into trouble, but with no lives being lost. As there was little accommodation in Valdez at that time, the complete community offered to house and look after the people who were rescued from the boat.

After a very enjoyable hour or two, I wandered on doing a bit more shopping, some wonderful shops. One I came across I would term as an ex-army type shop, the sort chaps like (what another!). This place was like Aladdin's cave, quite wonderful. I even managed to buy another native knife, plus more t-shirts. How ever am I going to get all this home? Finally, after lots of fuddling, I very reluctantly left the shop. I made it back to the motel and got stuck into my washing, sitting in my shorts, reading my native Alaskan book, whilst the washing whirled around and around.

Finishing my washing, I got spruced up and headed for the eating place/Oscar's. This was a very slow and enjoyable meal. The place was quite busy and I noticed the captain of the fishing boat we had been on. He said that the fishing wasn't good today - well, my silver was fine! "It's the weather you know" - don't think he remembers my enormous silver. I was planning on doing a little more fishing when I got to Seward - it was great!

I then walked slowly back to the motel, taking in all that was going on, people having BBQs, little family parties, boats of all shapes and sizes. I stopped and chatted - so very enjoyable. Sadly I turned and made it back to the motel. I must sleep, as I have a very early start - needed to be at the ferry by 7.00 a.m. I asked Reception to call me at 5.30 a.m. and then crawled into a wonderfully comfortable bed.

CHAPTER 26. FERRY and TRAIN TO WHITTIER VIA PRINCE WILLIAM SOUND

As always, I slept well. The phone was ringing....answer it.....oh no, I had just gone off to sleep (I thought!)......it was my early morning call! I was soon up and out, washed and shaved and off to the breakfast bar, having a cup of tea and a little to eat. I finished my breakfast and carried my few bits to my trusty steed, loaded up, finished putting my gear on and fired up the big single, having a look around and taking just a few more photos. The weather was nice so it should be a pleasant trip.

As I arrived, the ferry was unloading - just 2 lorries and a few cars. I stopped my bike and sat watching the proceedings. A rather large, strong looking lady was directing operations, but she did me proud and held up the cars and loaded me first! I parked my bike and looked around for rope to tie it down. I asked the lady for some and she turned out to be quite high ranking and did most things on the boat. She appeared with a small length of rope and I tied the bike to the bulkhead, then a car parked very close to me, well not a car, a four-wheel drive thing that would take the kids to school and also race across the desert (I was to find out later just how close it was). I found my way up and onto the deck and had a wander around, finding the lounge full of lower 48s watching TV. This is one of the most picturesque parts of Alaska and these people are watching TV - can you believe this? I can't. Well maybe they do this every day, who knows. I wandered onto the upper deck and found a seat. I sat and just looked.

The ferry set off, slowly moving away from its mooring and into the Sound. I could see the large mooring places where the big tankers sit to be loaded. It's a very large operation and very interesting. How can a country lad take all this in? I can't, so I kept taking the photos. The lady who had loaded us was now helping with breakfast. She had recognised my accent and wanted to chat as her mother was English. She also said we might see some whales, perhaps some orcas.

After my breakfast and a chat to the waitress, who also had British relatives, I was back on deck with my binoculars, scanning the coastline from each side of the ship as well as keeping an eye on the water around the ship. My first sighting was a sea otter with its baby on its chest. It was just bobbing along in the waves. I was also spotting many bald eagles. The ferry then seemed to quicken its pace as we cleared Valdez. The scenery was just so wonderful. (Pinch, pinch, am I really doing this?).

We had been moving for about an hour when the ferry slowed dramatically. I was scanning the skyline with my binoculars when I noticed what I thought was a great wave in the distance. This turned out to be an ice flow, which explained the reduced speed of the ferry. As we approached the flow the ferry again reduced speed, slowly edging through the ice field. We were now into large icebergs, floating each side of the boat. I had thought that the ferry cost was quite expensive, now I'm thinking "well worth every penny"!

In between all this beautiful scenery was food, a nice light lunch, some sort of cheese thing. Also another waitress told me her mother was English - what another?! We struck up a conversation about where her mother lived in England and how she had been planning to visit for the last ten years but had not yet got around to it. She lived in Juneau and said I must visit next time I was in Alaska. She also informed me that the large lady who loaded us onto the ferry was also the bursar and would like a chat about her British roots. We arranged to meet at tea time, about 3.30 p.m. I went back to my wonderful scenery, again trying to take it all in. I spotted a small colony of Stella sea lions, some diving into the water, some sunning themselves. They seemed to be light brown in colour - a sight to see.

Back for tea at 3.30 p.m. and my chat with the bursar about her feelings for England. She was enthusiastic but had no desire to return, telling me she had a little house in Juneau and was now quite settled. She had experienced several husbands, but was now happy with her dog (not a bad alternative!). We chatted for about an hour, when there appeared to be a problem somewhere on the boat so she took off and I returned to the upper deck - again trying to let this wonderful boat ride and scenery sink into my head. I was making the most of it as the journey was coming to an end, we were coming into Whittier.

We were called to go to the car deck and I went through the untying procedure. I straddled my bike waiting to move off. One of the seaman waved me forward and I engaged first gear and moved. I felt a bump and down I went. The car behind me ran into me! Two of the crew members ran to my assistance, they picked up my bike as I stood up. The pannier was off but apart from that, everything was fine. I wasn't hurt but I looked around at the asshole who had just done this to me and the prick was more interested to know whether or not he had marked his car. I muttered a few unsavoury words to him and then remounted. They held him back and let me ride off the boat.

As I left the ferry, I was directed to a parking area whilst the other vehicles were unloaded. The train arrived as this was going on. This was my next adventure.......

I was directed to the far end of the train (this is the train which takes you through the mountain). I rode to the end of the flat bed trucks, then up a ramp onto the train. It was a bit tricky getting on, especially with a large load on the bike then riding along the complete length of the flat bed trucks to the rear of the carriages. I was stopped by the guard and told to turn my bike around and tie it down to the bed of the truck. The turning wasn't the easiest of things to do but with a little manoeuvring I managed it. As I finished this exercise, a big cheer went up. I think everyone there must have been watching me! I was given some ropes to tie the bike down - if I messed this up I would certainly lose the bike. The job was completed - well it wasn't very satisfying as I had ropes everywhere - now fall off if you can!

After all this, I was able to look around. I was sharing my part of the truck with a lady kayaker, who told me she had paddled the same route as my ferry had taken - brave girl. She was about 25 years' old, looked very fit and must have a great deal of bottle to do that trip alone. We were just sat on the truck chatting when I noticed the prick who knocked me off my bike. In order to draw my attention to him, he stepped from his great big four-wheel drive thing and inspected his front wing for damage (obviously from the lower 48!). I didn't respond but left him to the little sad world he was living in.

The crew who ran the train seemed very nice and chatty. When the train was ready to move, I sat in the guard's van with my kayaking lady who gave me more details about her trip. I was all ears as not very often do you find a true adventurer - I think she is one. We also both put the world to rights, together with the guard! After our chats, we moved to more comfortable seats in the forward carriages.

I can't remember how long the train journey was, but it seemed very quick to me. I was soon out and untying my bike - it had survived! By the time I had the bike ready to move, all the cars had gone. I seemed to be running along the flat bed trucks for ages, finally reaching the ramp, carefully off and away - well that was some sort of trip.

Whittier was a strange place, there was something that looked like an old garrison type building, but which seemed abandoned and in need of tender loving care. You can reach Whittier by train or boat and there is also a landing strip. Whittier was created by the US Army during World War 2 as a port and petrol delivery station, in turn tied to bases farther north by the Alaskan railroad and later a pipeline. The railroad spur was completed in 1943 and Whittier became the primary debarkation point for cargo, troops and dependants of the Alaska command. Construction of the large buildings that dominate Whittier began in 1948 and the port of Whittier, strategically valuable for its ice free deep water port, remaining activate until 1960, at which time the population was 1200.

The 14 storey Begich Towers, formally Hodge, houses more than half of Whittier's population. The Buckner building, completed in 1953, was once the largest building in Alaska and was called the "city under the roof". It is now privately owned and is to be renovated. Whittier's economy is mainly the fishing industry and also increasing tourism.

(Thank you Milepost!)

I was now fired up and ready to head for Seward.

CHAPTER 27. SEWARD IN THE RAIN - AND MORE RAIN

I was on my way, heading towards Seward and was making good time as the road was tarmacadam and as yet no repairs, i.e. no stretches of gravel. The evening was setting in and , as I was about thirty miles from Seward, I decided to start looking for a camping place. I took to some dirt tracks, the third one was great and about 100 yards off the highway, there was a nice flat area to pitch the tent, with an abundance of firewood. The tent was soon up, the bedding in place, shelter fixed - quite high as I have found this to be a very important part of my camp as, quite often, mornings were wet and this enabled me to break camp without getting my gear wet.

I got the fire going and the tea on and then started the meal. It was tinned beans (American style), sausages and bread. This went down very well with a good mug of tea! During dinner, I was thinking of Seward the next day, but the weather was looking a little over-cast, in fact not looking too good. I was dropping off to sleep as I finished my meal. I think the sea, the wonder of it all, was just too much. I fell into my sleeping bag and slept

I awoke next morning to the sound of heavy rain. I struggled out of the tent, got the fire going and the kettle on and decided to break camp straightaway as the weather was closing in. I would make a dash for the coast. I dropped the tent, again just wearing my shorts. All my gear was under the canvas sheet and was nice and dry. I got dressed and then dropped the sheet, folded it and fixed it to my bike. After stoking up the fire, I was ready, the only wet clothing were my shorts and they were packed with the sheet. The KLR fired up and I was away down the track. The road was quite good so I was able to move with some speed. The rain became heavier as I neared the coast, so heavy that visibility became poor and I slowed down dramatically.

As I arrived at Seward, it looked a 'wonderful'(!) place in the bad weather, as everywhere does when its like that. My first stop was breakfast and a wash and brush up, then feeling brighter I tucked into a large breakfast (over easy!), at the same time chatting to a rather attractive lady who was spending a short holiday sightseeing, as well as some time with her son whose accommodation, as she described it, was a little primitive to say the least. She hardly looked able to rough it - in fact I would think she had a great many problems in her life. I did try and lighten her day, but it was hard going, so the local newspaper took over. I was now well fed, shaved and somewhat cleaner and comfortably warm.

I had been experiencing some strange vibrations coming from the front end of the KLR and then I noticed that the steering head had come loose. I needed a repair shop, or to have the loan of some large spanners. I put my gear on, it was wet but bearable, and set off looking for a place, easier said than done, but after riding around for half an hour, finally found a rather dilapidated looking garage with a very accommodating owner. He couldn't help me himself, but was quite willing to lend me the tools for the job. This was in between eating his spare ribs, in their polystyrene container, which he would park anywhere. He would go to serve petrol, taking a bite on the way past, then park the container somewhere else, away again. In between all this happening, there was water coming through the roof. At one stage, his ribs took a liberal dousing of rainwater! He also dropped one on the floor but, after a slight dusting off, he devoured it - pretty hygienic! Whilst observing the delicate manners of my host, I managed to tighten my steering head. When I had completed my work, I thanked him very much. He wouldn't take a single penny. I thanked him again as I was leaving, when I noticed his ribs parked next to the toilet so I quickly put five dollars into the container and made a hurried exit.

I was away and the rain getting a great deal worse so I aimed for the port area, thinking I might go fishing. I parked my trusty steed and settled down in a café with a large mug of tea but by then I decided there was no way I was going to attempt going fishing in the weather conditions.

So, today, it appeared I was a little stuck. However, I had seen a hording advertising "Sea World", so I decided to spend the day there - I just hoped they had a roof on the place! I braved the weather and fired up my very wet friend, followed the signs and was soon parking the bike. I wandered in and stood dripping everywhere. The lady at reception was very nice and could see the predicament I was in. She told me to take my gear off and she would hang it over a radiator. This was good news. Having done this and finding the place was quite warm, I paid my entrance fee and set off in my t-shirt and jeans, the only dry ones I had.

I started off at a very slow amble to enable me to take this all in. It was very interesting and amusing at times. My first stop was the seals - I think they were showing off, ducking and diving, also swimming right up to the glass and just staring at me. (Well, had they seen a Gloucestershire lad before?!) They are great swimmers, very agile. I read the information about the environment and also about the amount of pollution that had accrued in the last few years, as well as the over-fishing. I saw skeletons of many sea mammals - whales, sea lions - again lots of information and detail about all that was living around the coast of Alaska.

Moving on, I inevitably arrived at the gift shop, so I bought a few post cards, sat and wrote them, whilst taking a cup of tea. I moved on again and came across more on the Exxon Valdez and the terrible environmental damage it did at the time and is still doing to this day, not only to animal life but fish stocks, in turn affecting seals and other creatures with regard to their feeding. It is thought that the young Stella sea lions are badly affected, being unable to find small enough fish to feed on. At a young age, they are unable to venture out into the open sea, as if they attempt this they are easy prey for the orcas or anything else that needs a good meal.

I finally arrived at reception and the thought of getting my wet gear on and riding a bike was not a wonderful prospect. It was obvious that the weather was not going to improve so I thought I might go back towards Whittier. My fishing trip was not going to materialise. I was just hoping for nicer weather1

The receptionist had done a great job with the gear - it was somewhat drier - so fully dressed, I thanked her and made it back to my bike. It was still throwing it down, so full wet gear on. I fired up the big single and left my dry and warm sanctuary, first switching my heated jacket on. Next I found a supermarket for food and water , buying chicken, beans, some fruit and bread. I packed it all in plastic bags and tied it to the back of my bike.

I moved off slowly as it was now throwing it down. The ride had to be steady, as visibility was very bad. About twenty miles out of Seward, I ran out of the rain (nice!), the pace picked up I started looking for a camping place - what should turn up but last night's camping spot so I pulled in, parked up, got the tent up - things went very well and the shelter was up.

Whilst this had been going on, I did something that could have been an enormous disaster. To keep my gear dry, I had draped it over my bike with the engine running (wrong decision). I think it had been ticking over for about half an hour when suddenly I heard the note of the engine change. I rushed over and could hear a hissing sound and quickly worked out it was coming from the petrol tank. I switched off the engine and then went to release the petrol cap. The pressure in the tank was so great it was almost impossible to stop the cap blowing completely open. With luck and a struggle, I managed to release the cap slowly, allowing the vapour to disperse. Once again, it was safe. What happened was that the heat from the engine had heated the petrol which had vaporised and was ready to explode. Had the engine note not changed, I wouldn't have recognised the problem. The bike would have blown up, maybe taking me with it, or I could have been badly burnt. A lesson learnt. Lucky boy.

I enjoyed my meal of chicken and beans, plus all the condiments I kept collecting! Then, feeling tired, I turned in.

I was doing my usual - slowly waking up, really not wanting to. Was it morning again? I think there's a problem - I sat up and realised what was wrong. Everything was wet through, sleeping bag, my clothes were floating in a puddle (great). As I crawled out, I found the outer door flapping in the wind. I then moved quickly to the canvas cover. . Right what next - get some dry clothes from my pannier. The dry stuff turned out to be wet stuff, the whole lot was wet. I made the decision to pack up and find the nearest roadhouse, dry out, eat and then decide the next move. I need a hotel.

The rain was now very heavy - well, this is Alaska. I packed up pretty quickly and made a move. Fortunately the big single sprang into life, first things first I switched on my heated jacket. What a Godsend this jacket has been. I was soon feeling the warmth creeping through. This was not the most pleasant of trips but I dug in and got the KLR talking to me. About 20 miles out, a roadhouse appeared. I parked the now doubly wet KLR and wandered in to be greeted by two very nice ladies who welcomed me with "oh my dear, get those wet clothes off". As I was peeling them off, they were hanging them by a great big wood burning stove. I took myself off to the toilets and had a wash and shave, having already ordered my breakfast. I re-appeared, feeling a great deal better, and sat down to an enormous breakfast being placed in front of me.

I waded through my breakfast and decided I needed a place where I could get my washing done - also a room. My map told me my next stop was Hope. The ride was about fifty miles up the highway. I had a chat to the ladies and they gave me all the information I needed on Hope. They also had some nice postcards so I bought a few and wrote to my children, who must be thinking whatever is he up to now. Then, it was goodbye to the ladies, who insisted I called again!!

CHAPTER 28.   ON TO HOPE

I fired up my trusty steed and was, once again, eating up the miles. This bike has done me well and I have no complaints – it's great.

My sights set on Hope, I pushed on. My aim was to get a room with a shower, plus find a laundry.

Hope is on the Kenai Peninsula, on the south side of Turn Again Arm and provides access to the area of Resurrection Creek. It's a great fishing and rafting place, wonderful country and one can soon find the wilderness and, in August, still find snow. It didn't take me long to find Henry's One Stop. It also had a shop complete with a very nice lady - "oh, my dear, what weather we are having, do come in". (oooh, at last a laundry and a nice room for the night).

The shop lady was most helpful, she showed me the machines and dryers and after changing some money for the machines, I got on with the day's chores. First the tent was strung out along the veranda, then I dealt with the laundry. Both panniers were emptied and all the clothes were soaking wet, so I spent a pleasant afternoon sitting in my shorts, feeding money into the machines and reading my newly acquired book on the natives of Alaska. The laundry was very warm and cosy so that to me was a bonus!

Towards evening, I had a complete wardrobe of dry, clean, sweet smelling clothes. Loaded up, I took myself to the room and 'cooked' in the shower. Shaved, washed and dressed, I was like a new pin. I was now ready to hit the town! The extent of the town is a few houses, a couple of shops, Henry's One Stop, one bar, and Tetoe's breakfast place.

I had a walk to the pub - it was a nice walk but the pub wasn't much. I then walked on towards the sea - this was more like it - a salmon run. I had my wonderful telescopic rod with me, so I settled down to a little fishing. I fished for about an hour and caught about ten nice pink salmon - I actually landed them! I kept the first two and put the others back. If only my boys could see this.

Well, I had caught dinner so I packed up and wandered back,

stopping at the pub for a quick one. I could then totally confirm that it wasn't a very nice pub and the beer not a lot better. I wandered back to Henry's to cook my fish on my BBQ. I realised I needed some tinfoil and maybe a lemon, so set off to see if I could find what I needed. I hadn't gone far, in fact about 200 yards, when I spotted this enormous RV - wow, wow, wow, look at that. Is that big or is that big? It was complete with a Range Rover attached to the rear-end, plus two quad bikes and a sun lounge with table and chairs! (I bet they have 2 toilets!).

As I approached this RV-cum-luxurious coach, a chap appeared at the door. Well should I say his cigar appeared first and he was attached to the other end! With my head doing a 180% I wished him a good evening and explained my predicament. "Gee man, are you Australian?" "No, English". "Oh, thought you were Australian". I then got the works on how he had been a modest oilman in Texas, retired and had been coming to Alaska for ten years so his wife could go panning for gold. I stood well back to save getting poked in the eye with his cigar! How wonderful to meet a real pioneer.

After convincing me how wealthy he was, the chap produced the tin foil and one onion. The window then opened and out came the sliced lemon! The lady turned out to be his wife, about fifty five years old, very heavily made up, but seemed very nice - another true pioneer. (Must take hours in the morning to do her make up. I bet she doesn't go out in the rain - well, all that plasterwork, must be heavy!). She gave me a 'cracking' smile and went back to her television. Well, what an experience, a real American pioneer of the 20th century. I gratefully said goodbye and went on my way, returning to cook my dinner. I put some lighter fuel on the coals of my BBQ , and then headed to the other end of the car park with it, away from the bike, lit it and hung around until it was going quite well, at the same time looking in amazement at what was entering the car park.

It was an old American bus, a school bus that had been painted in camouflage colours. It had a trailer attached which was as long as the bus, on which were two old Jeeps, one skidoo, a dredge and many many more very interesting things! Just a host of equipment. Although I was trying not to be seen to be looking - I was staring! As the two boys clambered from their bus, they noticed me, also spotting my bike. They came straight over and introduced themselves. I had just met Roger and Ben…… and little did I know it but the next few days were going to be fun! They said "you were in Dawson", "Yes" I replied. "we saw you making for the ferry about five days ago" (that was me).

So Roger and Ben told me why they were in Alaska. They had both reached fifty years of age and decided that enough was enough. Ben had told his wife and she had agreed that it was fine for him to go to Alaska for two years. He paid his mortgage off on his house, settled all outstanding bills and prepared for this adventure. He had been married 3 times and was also a Vietnam veteran. After Vietnam, he had been through a bad time and was very reclusive and didn't see any of his family for years. He had finally settled down with his present wife - she must be very understanding.

Roger had talked things over with his girlfriend and she also had agreed to his plan but was coming up to stay with them after 6 months as by then, they should have settled on a claim. She was to become the cook and look after them (can't see that working somehow). So Ben had left his wife, Roger his girlfriend, and they had arrived in Alaska with all this kit , from the lower 48. They intended to be gold prospectors for two years - two more pioneers. They were doing this trip on a shoestring, as I could see from the kit they had with them! We decided that we would have a drink together when they had settled in and we had eaten.

I wandered over to look at this wonderful equipment. They had done all the work themselves, even down to making their own trailer, even the paint job was theirs. This was more like it - not all pioneers had passed on. Fascinated with all this kit, I then remembered the BBQ.

Both Ben and Roger were bikers and wanted very much to try my bike - sorry boys, no insurance, no ride. So they left me to eat and said they were going for a beer. Down went the trailer ramp, off came a Jeep, it fired up and went careering off down the road - well can you believe this?! I was just finishing my salmon as they returned. This could be fun (what another bad head!).

We all settled around the table in my room and started into a good long chat. They were very enthusiastic over their adventure. Their intention was to buy a claim and work it for two years. They were quite well equipped, dredgers and things. Whilst all this chat was going on, quite a few beers were disappearing! They asked me if I would like to go panning in the morning and I readily agreed. During our conversation, it came to light that Ben was part American Indian and apart from gold prospecting, he also made knives. He disappeared to one of his transport vehicles, returning with a sack, which he tipped onto the tables - knives, lots of them. He was very gifted and had so many different shapes and sizes. I set about bartering - I had my mind set on some knives, also his veteran's hat. I ended up paying 20 dollars for one knife. I traded a sweatshirt for another. Try what I may, I wasn't going to get his hat! Ben was delighted with his Isle of Man t-shirt and I was delighted with my knives. There was just one problem - how was I going to get them home?! (Oh, sort it out later)......

After the bartering had finished and the beer was consumed, I considered this had been a good night. I was ready for my bed and I turned in and slept like a baby. What a wonderful bed - warm and cosy...................

Morning seemed to arrive so quickly and even the shower wouldn't wash my headache away. Ablutions done, I wandered to Tetoe's cafe. Tetoe himself was a Chinese gentleman, probably well past retiring age. He seemed a very popular gent as people returned to Hope every year to call at his café. I was tucking into my breakfast when Roger and Ben appeared. They had been looking at prospective sites (boys!).

They talked to one local chap, who seemed very knowledgeable about claims and it was looking good for them as he thought he could help them. In fact, there were several sites quite near that were for sale. It was arranged that they would meet up tomorrow and have a look at them. How do you tell one from another, what's good, what isn't? Don't know.

CHAPTER 29. PANNING FOR GOLD - AND FISHING!

Having eaten I was ready to go to the river, however, Roger said they couldn't give me a lift as the jeep was full of gear. At that, one of the local chaps said he would be more than happy to give me a lift. It was no trouble, in fact he said he would show me some good places for panning. I dashed back to the room, packed a small haversack, my pan and, of course, my fishing rod and then we set off. My driver was Alaskan and had lived in this area for many years, now living alone. I think he had had a stroke or some type of injury as he seemed very weak on one side and was inclined to stumble, but truly a great character. On the way, we passed his home, set back in the woods, great for summer but winter.....well!

After about seven miles of dirt road, we came upon Roger and Ben, already setting up for the day's work - you could see they were taking this very seriously - well they had two years of this in front of them. My driver gave me a lesson on how to pan. This was fine but he seemed so unsteady on his feet although he was still very enthusiastic. Finally, he left me with a very cheery "have a great time ". I think he was quite a lonely man.

I got my head down and got busy. This was quite hard work and I needed reading glasses because should I find any gold it was likely to be so small that it would be very difficult to spot it! I stuck at it for about an hour, also having instruction from another lady who seemed very knowledgeable - rather like Jane, who I met at Denali. I did find a small amount, then gave up.

In my wisdom, I decided I was going to feed us all! Roger got the fire going and I was dispatched with instructions to catch salmon. As it happened, we were on a salmon run and I have to say I found fishing far more enjoyable than panning! Within ten minutes, I caught my first red salmon, cleaned it and cut the head off and took it back to Ben who was appointed cook. I wandered back to have another go - apparently we needed more! Well, tall order, so I set to work - oooh what fun. Within half an hour, I had three pinkies, gutted and headless. I took them to the cook who was very surprised - "just skill" said I! Ben explained that because reds are a little greasy it's better to cook them on a stick. The stick is cut into a 'V', stuck in the ground and just kept off the flames - this would allow the fat to run off, making the salmon drier to eat. Sounded good to me!

Back to my fishing. ....I then had another call "need another fish" - this is getting beyond a joke. Apparently we were now feeding the lady prospector, so being the modest chap that I am, I hooked another! I had had enough of this so I delivered it complete, head, guts, eyes, the works and passed it to Ben who grabbed it and, in a trice, had it topped, tailed and on a stick. Very impressive. We tucked into the cooked ones and they were very nice, compliments to the cook - first class job.

We all sat around chatting and eating, the subjects being gold, fishing and travel, also talk of England and my home. They were quite unable to take in that my little home was 500 years old. I had a picture with me that caused even more disbelief. In turn I found their past life and, indeed, present, most fascinating. These two were voted my best American adventurers yet - not only pioneers, but great characters.

After lunch, I fished for a while and the lads came over and had a go but, unfortunately, didn't catch any. This made my fishing look very professional! We finally packed up for the day - my only way back was very squashed in the back of the Jeep. This, as the lads had predicted, was a very uncomfortable ride. The walk back would have been great but I would, most likely, have arrived back at the Henry's next morning in time for breakfast!

The weather had been good all day so I intended doing a bike ride in the evening. I had talked to one of the locals in the café at breakfast and he had told me about a dirt road, about thirty miles long - apparently a most picturesque area (what's new?!).

By the time we arrived back at Henry's, I was feeling quite sick and glad to be released from the back of the Jeep. I thanked Roger and Ben, made it to the room and dived into the shower . Feeling more human, I got changed, put the kettle on, and had a cuppa .

I put my gear on and went down to the shop as I needed a couple more spinners - I always carry my fishing rod with me. I had a chat to the lady in the shop who was very interested in my adventures - she wanted to visit England - they all do!

The weather had been good so far and no dark clouds around. I straddled the big single and fired it up - so nice to be back in the saddle again, must be rested. I set off following the route we had taken this morning, then taking a left some four miles in. This was the old mining road I had discussed with the local chap this morning - just as described - beautiful and enhanced by the warm sunny day. It was a slow ride because there was so much to see as I moved up the valley. When I came to this wide area with seats, I parked up and took more photos of the scenery, eventually moving on up the valley. The road went to a narrow track, at the same time becoming stony and very wet in places.

I came across beaver performing in the lakes alongside the track. The track narrowed again and my thoughts now were what if a bear was on the track, I couldn't even turn around (scary). The local people had said there were quite a few about - in fact, some little while ago, a lady was walking with her two children and they had rounded a corner and stumbled upon a grizzly with a kill. It immediately attacked, killing the mother and daughter, the little boy ran and stumbled down a steep bank and rolled and rolled. The bear didn't follow and the boy survived.

A chap who I had also been in conversation with at Tetoe's had told me that when he was younger, he was out walking with his wife, and after parking his truck, but leaving his gun in it, they came upon a grizzly and two cubs. They had managed to climb a tree but the bear did everything it could to get them down. Finally, with his wife screaming constantly, the cubs wandered off and as soon as Mum missed them, she took off. When the bear was out of sight, the man left the tree and ran like the wind to his truck, grabbed his gun, ran back to his wife only to find the bear there again. He shot the bear and saved his wife's life - he said he had never realised a woman could scream for two hours. He did say he was sorry about the cubs, as they would never survive without their mother.

The track was very narrow now - I couldn't turn the bike around so I went steady , picking my way along. The fords were a little concerning as I couldn't see the bottom. There were also quite a few large rocks waiting for me to run into. As I progressed, it was getting colder and I was running into snow, then I came upon the remains of an old mine, or rather the remains of the buildings. I stopped, parked the bike and had a wander about. There was a great deal of steel about, some sort of rails I think, also very large lumps of wood, some bolted to the ground. How they got them this far was a mystery to me, they could have used horses I suppose.

Looking at the track again, it was becoming very steep, also with loose shale. I decided to go on, still having to pick my way, at times keeping the power on because the shale was moving, as well as manoeuvring around rocks. This now became a fight with the bike and the track which lasted for about fifteen minutes. Finally the track levelled out and I was able to stop. I decided it was time to go back and I knew I had to turn the bike around, but all the time I was thinking how could I do this as the track was so narrow, with a very big drop on one side. My first thought was to ride on until I could find a place to turn but as I looked ahead, I could see the track far into the distance and it was narrow all the way. I decided to turn around by trying to under-power and pop the front wheel up on the bank, then rock it backwards and forwards on the engine. If my footing went, I was straight down the bank and I couldn't have retrieved the bike from down there, even if we had both been in one piece.

I fired it up -" go for it". The wheel popped up, I rolled back, forward again, back, forward and as it finally came around I was looking down the valley, the fear now being could I lay it into the bank. Got it! I sat for a while, feeling a bit weak at the knees - it wasn't the bike that was worrying me, but the drop down on the other side. I gingerly moved forward, got my balance (good I'm away), arrived at the brow of the hill, stopped and peered down. I moved off, slipping and sliding, trying to keep the shiny side up, and made it safely to the mine. I stopped for a few minutes to catch my breath and then set off making my way down the valley, stopping for more photos and just taking in the scenery as I went. I was well down the valley when I met more adventurers on their way up - Roger and Ben in their Jeep.

As I neared Hope I found a wonderful viewpoint and got some great pictures - it was where the land meets the sea. Fabulous view. Eventually I moved on and finally joined the main dirt road to Hope and Henry's one stop. This was my last night in Hope before moving on to Anchorage and I think a little celebration was on the cards. I had a few beers with Roger and Ben and the little party went on well into the night. (What another headache…oooh!)

I slept very well. I awoke - with a headache! So this was to be a very slow start, slow shower, slow packing and slow drift to breakfast at Tetoe's. The boys were tucking into their breakfast when I arrived and after a hearty greeting (ooooh!), I sat down to a large mug of tea, followed by a very large breakfast. There was a lot of chat from the local boys as well as Roger and Ben, who were off to look at some claims. Before I had finished breakfast, the boys got up to leave, so there were goodbyes from everyone.

It was sad, as we had all had a great time.

CHAPTER 30. BACK TO ANCHORAGE - MY FINAL STOP

I finished breakfast and got straight out, wishing everyone the best. I was away. I dropped the key into the shop and walked to my trusty steed, fired up the big single and pointed it towards Anchorage. I needed some miles under my belt. Well, I hadn't gone far when I came upon cars parked everywhere. I pulled up on the bridge, looking down to the river to see many many fishermen - must be a salmon run. I parked the bike and just stood on the bridge, watching this spectacle and they were certainly hooking them out. I tried to get some photos but the camera was playing up again - I took some anyway just hoping for the best. Should I get the rod out? No, it was a bit too crowded, thinking of the Copper River when there was just me.

I fired the bike up and away again, the weather was holding and I was back on tarmacadam roads with traffic and people. It felt very strange. I had been used to so much wilderness and now everything was so busy with cars and people! The riding was good and as always I was buzzing, also singing as usual. However, I do like the tracks and the quietness of it all, having never ridden on dirt, I had quite surprised myself.

About mid-afternoon, I rolled into Anchorage - now this was busy. First things first, lodgings. I tried the Youth Hostel, that was full. So, I went looking and even though it was for three nights only, I felt I needed comfort. I came across the Inlet Inn, just off the centre. Good parking and not the best of rooms (so not so spoilt after all then!). The chap at reception put me in the room behind the 'winking' hotel sign - well, anyway, it was warm with a bath, so it would do.

I unloaded my bike, took all the stuff to the room and then unpacked the lot. The bike was now ready to return to the rental place tomorrow. I had used my stuff sack for the last four weeks so was able to repack some of my gear - this bag had worked out fine, but was looking a little worse for wear (a few holes).

I rang Tom, the bike hire man, and arranged to return the bike the next day. I had packed most of my gear, now it was time to walk. I stepped outside. Well....Anchorage, a city, civilisation. I wandered into the centre and found a nice restaurant and settled down for my meal. The problem I had was the number of people there were around, back to reality! Well, not really, it's quite interesting just to sit and look. I took my time over my meal! Now quite comfortable, it was time to shop - and very interesting shops they were. I found a great sports type camping shop (a boy's shop!). I bought a Leatherman with Alaska engraved on it for my son, also a nice sweatshirt (what another one!!).

Shopping done, I stopped at a bar for a pint and got into conversation with a very talkative and interesting native Alaskan. He told me about his hunting in the winter and about his family who lived in the north. I asked him if he returned to his family home - yes he did, but not for long as he missed his home comforts in Anchorage, heating, TV, a bath (spoilt lad!!). It was great listening to him.

I left the pub and walked back to the hotel . I turned in - I was getting used to these things called beds - and enjoying them! I slept like a baby, but I found waking up in a dark room was very strange. I was used to waking up with so much light - not much to stop it in a tent. However, a shave and shower soon put it right. Next breakfast.

I found this rather nice bar, just a little bit up-market to what I had become accustomed to, but fine. Well, this is the city! The waitress didn't ask how I wanted my eggs as she walked away with my order, strange, so I said "over easy please". After breakfast, I walked back to the hotel and put my gear on to set off for Tom's place. I had to make the best of this ride on my KLR, which had been a trusty steed. I fired it up and was away. I was making good time as the roads were tarmacadam - fast. Once again the big KLR was talking to me. I got very close to Tom's home, but couldn't find it. I rode around for a while and then got totally lost, eventually stumbling upon a Musk Ox farm, complete with guided tours. (OK, why not?!).

So, it was off with the gear and I followed the guide who took me to all the different pens. I was thoroughly enjoying these wonderful animals.

They are like buffalo, big boys. The guide told me it was the rutting season and I could see from the performance of some very large males that they were certainly playing up! In the shop you could buy the musk ox hair, which I think was for spinning, also garments made from the hair of these magnificent animals. The garments were expensive, but very nice. However, I wouldn't want to comb one of the males at this present time!

After this unplanned visit I moved on, again looking for Tom's place. I found the main road, but just couldn't find the turning to his house. However, I did find a roadhouse and decided to have lunch. I could then phone Tom and get directions. So, after parking my bike, I rang him, to find that I was only about half a mile from his house! Well, that's fine. I walked into the roadhouse and there was just the waitress - no-one else (bit worrying - wonder what the food is like?). I ordered just something simple - the waitress was very chatty and talked all through lunch!

Now, wanting to move, I wished her the best and went on my way, soon arriving at Tom's. It was a nice day, so we sat around chatting and I gave Tom my route and he said he would check out some of the places I had visited, also the roadhouse at Talkeetna. He said he would let them know I had returned in one piece.

Finally, I had to say goodbye to my big KLR and be on my way. I have never been an off-road rider, but I had enjoyed the KLR and the dirt roads and tracks. Tom took me back to Anchorage in his truck, and it was yet another sad goodbye. The bike had cost me a lot of money, but it had been worth every penny. Yes, I had fulfilled a life's dream. The great thing was I wanted to do it again.

Little did I know what was in store for me in the very near future.......................

I stepped out of Tom's truck at the hotel, thanked him very much and promised to keep in touch. (I have actually kept in contact with Tom in Alaska, by email).

I was away to my room to get changed - I had phoned Jane, the lady I met panning for gold, who lived in Anchorage and she had invited me to go for a meal with her - she would pick me up at my hotel. She eventually arrived and it was nice to see her again.

I climbed into her pickup truck and she drove me across Anchorage and it was quite enjoyable being able to take a good look around. Leaving the city behind us, we pulled into a large parking area, with only us in it. The restaurant was quite interesting, just a large wooden building, nothing like an English restaurant (well it wouldn't be, its Chinese!) I followed Jane to the door. She was obviously a regular customer, as the lady greeted her as you would an old friend - and, yes, we were their only customers. I wondered how they made it pay with so few of customers all evening as, whilst we were there, no one else came in. However, both the wine and the meal were excellent.

Jane said that she had stayed at her camp (panning for gold) a little longer than originally planned. Her brother had been worried about her and had asked the police to check her out. They sent an officer out to look for her but by the time he caught up with her, she was on the move. The officer had eventually stopped her and said her brother was worried about her and would she ring him. The policeman had driven fifty miles to look for her - not bad service. Jane said he was very nice and had referred to her as "young lady"!. I think she is sort of middle age but I found her very interesting and quite fun.

She told me a little about her work. She works with climbers who have had accidents and have been rescued from the mountains of Alaska. She was currently nursing a pair of English lads who had frostbite, one had some toes removed and the other most of his fingers, oooh. Jane had very strong views on climbers, her reasons being that so many groups run into trouble and get frostbite. In the case of the two British lads, one, in time, will be able to walk with difficulty (he had lost some toes) and nothing will show, but the other one's life will be hard. Everyone can see his disability and he will be very limited as to what he can do as he has no fingers. I think she feels they put themselves in jeopardy, plus it costs so much to nurse them back to some sort of normality.

We chatted about my adventures in Alaska; I think Jane was delighted

I had actually survived! She gave me her address - this would enable me to return to Alaska, perhaps fly a bike in and she would store it until I arrived. She also said it would be no trouble to get me a gun before I arrived. All the local people I had talked to say they would not camp in the wilds without a gun - so that was good enough for me. My intention was to return to Alaska.

Jane dropped me off at my hotel and I then walked to the local bar for a pint of Guinness. This went down very well. I had a chat to a few others at the bar and then, finally, wandered back to the hotel and fell into bed after searching for my reading glasses - I think I may have packed them.

CHAPTER 31. MY FINAL DAY IN ANCHORAGE

The next morning was dark as always in the room behind the sign, so I decided to find some tea and perhaps breakfast. I made it up the street and followed my nose into a hotel and then into their breakfast bar. This was a very nice place and I settled down to a pot of tea, ordering my breakfast - as usual "over easy"! The chairs were comfortable so I sat with the local newspaper, trying desperately to read the small print. (I really must find a store that does 'readers'). When the waitress arrived with my breakfast, I asked her if she knew where I could buy a pair of glasses. "Oh, yes, J C Penny's, they sell them". She told me it was about two blocks away and gave me directions. Breakfast over, I thanked her, paid my bill and left.

I walked the two blocks and found the backdoor of J C Penny's - this place was great, not a gift shop, but a store. I would think this is where the Alaskans shop. I wandered around and made enquiries as to where the Spec department was. "Top floor, sir". I beetled off to the top floor where I found the department, empty apart from the assistant and myself. I looked at the selection of specs, decided on a cheap pair which I was able to read with. Great, that sorted me out and I went to pay the lady. I produced my credit card which she put through the machine - it was promptly refused. She tried it again and again it was refused. "I'm sorry, sir, but you will have to go to the customer help desk". She directed me a few yards to another desk where I then spent the next hour trying to convince them that I had used my card in Alaska for the last month, so there was no reason why it shouldn't work. Finally, they rang the card company direct - good. They confirmed that the card was OK so finally they put it through and it worked. Glasses secured, I made my way slowly through the store, finding the clothing department very interesting! I found the shirt rack - I fancied one with a tartan pattern and lining, sort of winter job. I tried several on, finally decided on a dark green, "Original Alaska", great, that was what I wanted. I handed over my credit card and, with fingers crossed, it went through. I then drifted through the store, looking at the things you can't buy in England (most of it). I was so enjoying J C Penny's.

I decided I needed some cash just to last me the day and found a bank on the ground floor of the store. I had a go at the cash machine, or should I say several goes. I was getting no where and the queue behind me was getting longer. I apologised to the lady behind me and she passed it along the queue, saying "he's English!". I did then hear a few comments! Now, I stood no chance, as they were all becoming agitated. I did hear "tell the prick I haven't got all day" !!

I left the cash machine and went into the bank and joined the queue. I finally reached the cashier, having observed the people in front of me and their very strange behaviour - or so it seemed to me. They all seemed very abrupt and not really very pleasant to the lady who to me appeared to be very nice and doing her best. Finally I reached the desk and was greeted with "Hi". She was a dark lady, about twenty eight years old, and very helpful. I explained my problem and she took my card, picking up the phone to check my details. During the call, she quizzed me about home. She cleared the card and asked me how much I wanted.. I said about 30 dollars. Apparently the minimum amount was 50, which was obviously why I had had a problem at the machine. She said "would you like me to do the exchange for you"?. I said "Yes, great idea" which saved me messing about with the machine again - and who could guarantee I would get any money out of it any way?!

She was very quick and soon handing the 50 dollars over to me. She bade me a joyful farewell and I was soon out and drifting down the road, complete with my wedge of money.

I decided to go to the bus station to enquire about a ride to the aircraft museum. It turned out to be very cheap but as I was walking towards the station I was thinking who wants to ride for an hour on a smelly bus when one could walk around the town on a beautiful sunny day like this, or even perhaps a walk to the river (what more fishing!). I left the station and walked across town, taking in a little shopping on the way. I found a most interesting ex-army, sports, camping, fishing and hunting type shop, with a wonderful display of Leatherman knives. I studied these with my new glasses in position!

Gosh I can see the fine detail. I also spotted a very nice Buck knife but decided against buying it as it was too expensive for me. However, after leaving the shop, I returned within five minutes and purchased it for myself!

I walked on and found myself near the railway line, which I followed for a few hundred yards. I crossed over to the riverside and continued until I arrived at the old station, when I found the station pub (for the life of me I can't remember its name). I walked in and found they sold a great deal of different beers. I sat on the veranda, the sun was very warm and I was beginning to like this leisurely life. The waitress arrived and once again we were chatting about England, whilst she showed me the selection of beers. I chose a very dark beer (wonder why?!) and ordered a prawn salad. My waitress had an accent but what it was I couldn't make out and quite forgot about it during our conversations.

The beer arrived and, yes, it was a very enjoyable drink (I may have another!). My lunch arrived and I took my time eating it and every time the waitress came to serve a new customer, she would stop and we would carry on our conversation - well this is nice. Whilst resting and taking the sun, I emptied my travel wallet of pamphlets and receipts, keeping the good stuff, i.e. cards and things I had picked up on my travels. I also had a look at my purchases of the day - my Buck knife, my wonderful Alaskan shirt - I was checking it out when I noticed the label "made in China". Oh well, I thought, it looks like the proper job - it's a treasure - just cut the label off!!!

Finally, feeling quite rested, I wished my waitress farewell and started to wander back towards the town. Within minutes, I met a lad carrying three very large salmon. "Where did you catch those?" I asked, "just over there" he said, pointing to the river. OK, instant decision, I'm going fishing. I turned again, heading for the town, stopping to buy a licence and some spinners, also a couple of t-shirts for my son. I arrived back at the hotel and grabbed my rod, back to the river where I found a spot I could squeeze into. It was great fun, so many people enjoying themselves, some very serious fishermen, some not so serious. It was great. My biggest problem was I kept getting my line tangled up with other lines. Two amateurs tangling up were fine but when you tangled with a professional, it was quite different - they don't like it! Quite a few fish were being caught, in fact a girl just up from me caught four in about ten minutes. I did get one bite and this spurred me on. I was so intent on my fishing that I didn't notice the water level rising, until my boots filled up. Oh well, it was warm wet!! I kept at it, forever hopeful, but I had a feeling that the girl next to me was catching mine. I stuck at it for another hour, but having caught nothing and with the water turning cold in my boots, I packed my trusty rod and wandered back to the hotel, dreaming about the one that got away and the great day I was having in Anchorage.

Back to the hotel, showered and spruced up, I set off, first calling at reception to organise an early morning call and a taxi to the airport the next day. I settled my bill and took off to the local bar and eating house. It was very busy but I managed to get myself a pint of Guinness, but there was no where to sit. I ordered a pizza, at the same time looking for a seat with a table. I was chatting to one of the chaps who were playing in the band, well more like shouting at him. His mother was English, so he talked about his relatives in England and how he was planning to go to England next year to play in a band.. He said the band had been at the Blue Grass Festival at Talkeetna, that was why there were so many bands in town for the past few days.

As he returned to his band, he said "do stay and enjoy the evening" - this I readily agreed to do, well it was my last night in Alaska! I finally grabbed a table, at the same time ordering another pint. My pint arrived within two minutes and I promptly returned it to the barmaid, who was shocked. I explained how I would like it poured - s l o w l y! I asked her to start pouring my second pint as soon as I had started drinking my first, so she agreed to try it. From then on, they came slowly - and good. During the evening she got the hang of it as I had some great pints. My pizza arrived - it was enormous. However, I believed I could do it justice!

The band took a rest and my friend was back over chatting, at the same time helping himself to my pizza - well it couldn't be just for one man! The band struck up again and got into good country music and I was very much enjoying myself. Another member of the band came over and was chatting/shouting! He apparently had his own group, but had just come for the Blue Grass Festival at Talkeetna. I had heard about the festival but was too busy with my adventure to be able to go to it. I would like to go - perhaps when I come to Alaska next time. One would like to do everything, but there is only one problem - TIME.

I had another pint or two. My barmaid loved it and had relayed the story to some other Guinness drinkers and they were getting the same treatment. The band finally stopped about 12.30 and, after having another chat to the lads, I said my farewells and went on my way, bouncing past the two bouncers on the way out, who kindly pointed me in the right direction!!

I made it back to the hotel. I wandered past reception, asking again for an early morning call, probably realising I would definitely need it. I got to my room and fell into bed.

CHAPTER 32. GOODBYE ALASKA

What the hell is that noise? It's the 'phone, it can't be I've only just got into bed. Wrong, it was morning, oooh….. I crawled out, showered and shaved and was off down to reception. The taxi was already waiting and the driver started to load my bags. He was a coloured chap about six feet tall, strong boy. We set off in the direction of the airport - well at least that was the way we were supposed to be going. It wasn't long before I realised the taxi driver was pissed and at about the same time his taxi started misfiring. Finally, we came to a halt about a mile up the road.

Oh dear, I think we have a problem!! The driver can't stand up and now the engine won't go. He sat there for five minutes turning the engine over until the battery ran flat - great. He then had the sense to ring the Control and, fortunately, another taxi turned up. I bundled my bags into the second taxi and left my original taxi driver, drunk, with no engine. The new driver was a lady and native Alaskan - thanks to her I arrived at the airport in good time - no thanks to my drunken friend.

I unloaded, paid up and wandered to the Check-In, handed my ticket to the lady at Departures, together with my bags, then found the gate I would be leaving from. Once that was established I headed off for breakfast . Eventually, the final call came, my flight was boarding.

Just as I was entering the tunnel, I turned. Alaska I will return. I waved goodbye……..

CHAPTER 33. RETURN TO ENGLAND

I left the airport departure lounge at Anchorage, walked along the tunnel and boarded my flight home. I managed to get my helmet stowed away then took my window seat. There was the usual buzz of everyone getting seated. I think I was asleep before the plane even took off! The next thing I knew was the lady sitting next to me was telling me the meal was coming. I ate my meal and immediately fell asleep again.

We stopped at Minneapolis to re-fuel and, just to kill time, I shopped, but I wasn't very interested in the inflated prices and the abnormality of it all. I had a wash and brush up and very shortly after that they were calling my flight. I boarded, found my seat and settled into the long flight home. I read a little, ate a little, as you do, but mostly I slept!

Finally, the pilot announced we were approaching Gatwick - it was about 7.30 a.m.

We landed and I was soon into the luggage terminal, grabbed my bags, then legged it to the coach station where I purchased a ticket to Heathrow, found my coach and settled in.

We set off but to my surprise we didn't go on the M25, but took what appeared to be a back route and, in no time, we arrived at Heathrow. As I was unloading my bags, I saw the coach I needed just pulling out of the station - I'd missed it - so, a cup of tea and wait for the next one. I struck up a conversation with a young chap who was telling me he had just arrived from South Africa, where he had been playing rugby. He was now heading home and was hoping to get signed up by a very prominent Welsh team.

Just on the hour the coach pulled in, the driver helped me load my luggage and I found a double seat so I could stretch out properly and sleep. Having already spent hours in a cramped position on the long flight home, this was luxury! Once again, I settled down and slept - I think I must have been catching up after very little sleep and lots of action on my holiday. I woke as we were skirting around the town nearing my destination and gathered my hand luggage as the coach pulled into the station terminus. Out again, the driver passed me my luggage and I deposited it onto the pavement.

Right, next, make a phone call to my son, I thought, but there was a problem as I hadn't any English money - nothing, as I'd spent my last pound on a drink at Heathrow. I couldn't carry my luggage very far so I stopped the first lady who came by! I explained I had just arrived from London, having travelled a long way and I hadn't got a bean to phone anyone to get a lift home. The lady immediately handed me 20p and said "I've always wanted to go to Alaska", so I chatted with her and answered about twenty questions about my holiday. Finally, she went on her way, accompanied by many thanks from me. I was making a beeline for the phone box when, amazingly, I bumped into a chap whom I had worked with a few years previously. Well, how convenient was that! He had just stopped to use the toilet. I explained my predicament and he said he would drop me in town, so with all my gear stowed into his car, we took off and within minutes we arrived at the drop off point. Gear unloaded, again, we had a little natter and he went on his way.

I telephoned my son, who was delighted to hear from me and was soon arriving to pick me up. Delighted to see one another we headed home. I unloaded my presents on him and then dived into the bath. With a struggle, I managed to keep awake that evening before finally retiring to bed for a very good sleep.

CHAPTER 34. BACK TO WORK

I started work again for two days, then it was the weekend. I had found my two days' work quite hard - I was probably suffering from jet-lag. Driving back after work I 'dropped off' twice which wasn't very good - there was no warning, my head just dropped. I was lucky - the first time it happened, the van brushed the side of a hedge and the second time I missed a wall. However, I did manage to get to the Friday night when I was off to the pub with my son and another friend. We had a great evening and I relayed some of my stories of my holiday. Saturday morning I wasn't feeling quite so good but I enjoyed my weekend, seeing friends and relaxing.

Monday morning, back to work and then, after a couple of days, I moved to a job on the farm of a regular customer. I was working on some lights, with my ladder next to my van. Opposite was a grain store and whilst I was working there , some very large tractors with big trailers were coming in, dumping their loads then heading out again to the fields and the combine harvester, to collect more grain.

During all the comings and goings, my mobile phone rang. I came down the ladder and was talking to my son, at the same time standing next to my van.

From now on I have no memory of what happened. Most of the information has been supplied by other people. Latterly, I can tell my own story. I have since found scraps of paper with notes on which have also helped me to write this. Some things I do remember but they have taken time to come back to me.

-----------oOo----------

PART TWO

CHAPTER 35.   THE ACCIDENT

One of the tractors came into the shed opposite. It dumped its load...
and then the driver forgot to lower the tailgate on the trailer, therefore
doubling the height of the trailer itself. He left the shed and the tailgate
caught the feed pipe that conveys the grain to the transport lorries. That
pipe was 14 feet long and weighed 2 cwt. It was thrown across the road,
hitting me on the right side of my head, also pushing me into the van,
causing further damage to the left side of my head.

Farm workers were running towards me, someone phoned for an
ambulance.

I was unconscious but apparently tried to get up and had to be held
down by one of the men. They tried to stop the bleeding but with little
success. The general opinion was that I wasn't going to make it.

The farm manager arrived and things started to move. The
ambulance arrived and the medics set to work on me, also getting me into
the ambulance - the farm manager said it seemed an age before it finally
left.

At the same time as the ambulance arrived at Frenchay Hospital in
Bristol, my son also arrived. I was taken inside and immediately put into
the scanner. When I was removed from that, my son was told I had five
minutes left to live if the surgeons didn't operate straightaway. He
obviously gave them permission to operate immediately and the pressure
was released from my brain by putting tubes into my head.

My scull was smashed in. I was then taken to the Head Injury Ward.

How long after my accident it was, I don't know, but at some time I
knew that my children were there, but that's all. I didn't know that my
eldest son and daughter had been sent for from their homes in USA, as
the hospital thought I might not survive - they came immediately to be at
my bedside. Apparently, I would answer questions but I have no
recollection of doing so. My father came to see me and his opinion was
that I wasn't going to make it.

After a few days, I could recognise them, but not a lot else. I am told that the staff were wonderful, as was the surgeon who saved my life and the staff who nursed me. (I know now that they were all wonderful and I return to the ward every year with small gifts. I did this from the first year when someone took me there, then a few years later I was able to go alone. One nurse said she recognised me - hard to believe as I was in a terrible state).

I have very little memory of my stay at Frenchay Hospital in Bristol.

CHAPTER 36. GLOUCESTER ROYAL HOSPITAL

After some time, there was discussion of me being moved to Gloucester Royal Hospital so, when the time was right, I had large clips removed from my head and was transported there by a specially constructed ambulance. It comprised of very special suspension, enabling the patient to feel nothing of the actual journey or road conditions.

I was in a small room of my own. My daughter and my two sons would visit me, also my partner, my father, my sister and friends. Apparently, I became quite chatty and enjoyed their visits but as soon as they had gone, I would have no memory whatsoever of them being there.

After a while, I was able to get to the toilet with the aid of two nurses. I was having great difficulty in moving my bowels, in fact it became quite serious and I was given everything imaginable to try and 'move' me. Finally, after days, the situation improved.   However, the problem persisted for many years but now, with a balanced diet, I have improved greatly, but I will never be the same again.

Any instruction I was given by the medical team at this time was forgotten by me in seconds. I was retaining nothing. Also my left side was numb from my head to my toes and I had a permanent headache, which persisted for two years before it started to ease.

It was quite easy for me to fall - and I did, often.

My stamina was very low and my biggest task was to sleep. Fortunately, I managed to sleep a great deal.

The next aim was to get me into a bath, which was obviously achieved with some difficulty, with the aid of a nurse. I was in the bath, wonderful, and then apparently I told the nurse I needed a wee. She said "well you can't get out now, so wee in the bath". I believe I did!!

I began to be a little more mobile and was able to make my way to the day room. Just off the day room were some stairs, only about six treads high, but used to help people to learn to walk up and down stairs again. I persisted with these stairs every day, wobbly but determined to master them. After some time, I succeeded, so then I was looking for a further challenge - wonderful. I graduated to making it to the staff canteen and getting a meal. I was found out and told that if I did it again I must have shoes on because I could bring germs back to the ward. I must also inform a nurse where I was going.....Oh dear!!

I don't know how I did this. I think it was because I didn't know why I was there, or had any feelings one way or another. I didn't realise what had happened to me, so there was never any thought that I wouldn't fully recover. However, as time went on, I developed a great fear at undertaking anything.

My days consisted of eating and sleeping and seeing visitors. Every time my son visited me (daily) I would ask him why I was in hospital. He would say because you have had a bad accident. Still no short term memory.

During all of this, my children were with me, in mind if not in body. My daughter and my eldest son were in America, but my youngest son was with me as much as he possibly could. My sister would come in to see me, but I have no memory of this.

Eventually, I was introduced to my Occupational Therapist. She was great and would sit and talk to me, about what I can't remember, but I felt great comfort from knowing that she was there for me and seemed to understand me. I did tests to see how I was progressing and she was indicating that they would soon be deciding if I could cope at home. It was decided that I should do a home visit. She said "you will be worn out when you come back". I thought "I don't think so"………

So, off we went in her car, arriving at my home. I saw my son - it was so good to see him and be home. The occupational therapist wanted me to try getting into the bath - managed that ok - then up the stairs and down the stairs - managed that ok as well. So far so good. Then I wanted to see my bikes so my son opened up my workshop and I sat on one of my bikes. It was great.

I was then taken back to the hospital and arriving at the ward I fell into bed and slept....and slept.......

I remained in hospital until they were ready to send me home. I never asked to go home. I thought "they'll send me home when I am ready".

I did more tests later in the Occupational Therapy department. I don't remember what they were but I guess they were to do with whether or not I was ready to go home.

CHAPTER 37. MY RETURN HOME

One day, my son arrived at the hospital and took me home.......

This was all very strange. I seemed to settle in to a very difficult way of life consisting of eating and sleeping but with no support, no one to lean on, no confidence. Mornings were particularly very hard. I would wake up to the room spinning with me clinging onto the bed - this persisted for a long time.

Walking was difficult as I would bounce off the furniture, fall, stumble. Sometimes I was good, sometimes very bad. This has slowly eased, but when I am tired it comes again. Rest stops it. Dizzy spells are an under-statement.

I could do nothing. I couldn't boil a kettle, cook anything. Then I found that I couldn't taste anything when eating. The dizziness was a big part of my life, continuing to walk into things and stumble along, making me feel very sick. I sat next to the roses in my garden to smell them, nothing. So....no taste and no smell......

My son decided to get me a computer. Trying to master it at that time was very difficult, to say the least, and I would sit and become very frustrated with it, but slowly, very slowly, I began to learn how to use it. (Now, I have great pleasure using it - writing, e-mailing and communicating with people). Learning wasn't easy and my frustration grew. I was then introduced to a chap, a computer man, who was to try and help me progress. I wasn't a nice person to deal with but, through it all, he was great and never seemed to get rattled with my ravings. He has stood the test of time and I feel now that he isn't a computer man but a friend - who sorts my computer out!!

Mornings continued to involve me getting up, clinging to the bed to try and stop my head from spinning. My partner helped me to get downstairs, where I used a small bed and would stay there most of the day. However, if I could climb the stairs in the afternoons, I would go to bed, sometime sleeping for four hours. Friends would arrive and get me up, get me downstairs again, and seated. I was very insecure, needing to lock myself away. My frustration grew. I had a friend doing some jobs for me and if they weren't completed when I thought they should have been, I would get very frustrated - I just wanted him gone when I was ready to sleep...............

Some weeks after coming home from hospital, I had a disagreement with my then partner and she left, leaving only her cat. I had become fond of the cat - she would sit by me.

The cat stayed for a few weeks then one day she was gone. I missed her very much.

I had no curtains on the ground floor of my house, so it wasn't nice at night, looking out into the blackness. At Occupational Therapy, they gave me some old curtains to nail to the wall. Eventually, I got some new ones and my friend put some curtain rails up for me.

Some time later, a very old friend, who some years later became my dancing partner, told me that she had thought that I wasn't receiving visitors when I was in the hospital; however she later spoke to my son, who explained to her what had happened. It was some time after when I realised this lady had not been to see me and I felt upset about this, obviously not knowing that she had tried to visit. Then, one evening, I bumped into her. I knew who she was but I couldn't move - she said her name over and over again and finally we locked in an embrace and cried together, not noticing anybody else who was in the room! It upset us both, but we are good friends again and see each other regularly.

There were many challenges when I was at my lowest ebb. Fortunately, my family and friends rallied round me. My son was always there, my sister would call and visit me, and my dear uncle and niece would visit. He gave me money that he had willed to me, as and when he passed on. He said "you need it now" - how right he was - it helped me so much.

I was always worn out after any visit, always needing to sleep.............................

CHAPTER 38.   THE LONG ROAD TO RECOVERY

Now living on my own, I was assessed for needs and it was decided that I should have some care support. This came in the form of care assistants for three mornings a week. Also, as I was unable to cook for myself, meals were delivered once a week.

The carer's job was to see that I got up and down stairs OK, to make my bed, bring in logs for the fire and tidy up - as well as to see that I was generally OK. They wanted to come and get me up on a morning and I know I fought this and would get myself out of my spinning bed and get myself dressed. Also I needed to sort out my eyelids which were always stuck together - I had to bathe my eyes to release the eyelids - a problem which persisted for about two years. I also had a problem with one ear, which constantly needed cleaning out - again it eventually cleared up. My scalp was constantly breaking out in painful spots - this problem took about five years to clear up. All these tasks had to be achieved each morning and then somehow I got down the stairs into my chair. However, it was a comfort to know that someone was coming in to see me. I was frightened at first, but settled down and eventually I think I looked forward to them coming.

I was always very tired, frightened of anything new in my life. My life went on but I was very lonely. I would crave company but when I got it, it was almost too much for me to bear and I would retreat into my private world or into what I thought of as my 'prison'.

Occasionally, if I was feeling well enough, I would go to the building next door - this was actually the office for my business which was adjacent to my house at the time. I would find our company secretary there and much to her alarm I would climb the stairs to see her, quite often falling down. Somehow, I knew she was there for me which was a comfort. I would ask how the company was doing, were the finances all ok, etc. and she would bring me up to date - and then I would promptly forget everything she had told me.

She was and is a good friend to me - and still our company secretary.

One day, my son decided to take me to the local town. This was a very traumatic experience for me. I was walking down the street with him and the people walking towards me weren't walking but **flying with flames coming out of their heads.** I was soon taken home. However, my experience of that day told me nothing, as it was all forgotten by the next day - no short term memory whatsoever.

So, life went on, just sleeping and eating very little food as I had no real appetite and couldn't taste anything. I had to have smoke alarms and a gas alarm fitted. (When I finally was able to cook, I had the most exercised alarms in the area!).

The placid man I once was, was gone. My anger grew with great frustration. I started to smash things. Suddenly, instantly, I would grab a plate, a cup or a dish and just smash it against the wall. I don't know how long it lasted but it was a long time, months even.

I was taken to see a specialist at Frenchay hospital and he asked my son if I was smashing things. "Yes", was his reply. The specialist turned to me and said "It doesn't matter if you smash the chairs through the window, you will stop" - and I did , after some time. It was a strange experience though as I would smash something, then feel good, go and get a dustpan and brush and happily clean up the mess.

My headaches persisted, accompanied by head clamps.

All the time, I was looking out from my own little world to another world outside, your world..........

CHAPTER 39.   OCCUPATIONAL THERAPY and HELP FROM 'LIFESTYLES'

Setting off to go to Occupational Therapy:
By ambulance -

Slowly, I continued my long recovery and it was decided that I should go to Occupational Therapy at Gloucester Royal Hospital. Very reluctantly, I agreed. I was picked up by an ambulance on the first morning and by the time I was half way to the hospital, I was very ill, frightened and distressed - we didn't go straight to the hospital as we were picking up other patients, bumping around all over the place - it was all just too much for me to take. Arriving at the hospital, I was put to bed and slept until it was time to leave for home.

By taxi -

From then on, I was taken direct to the hospital in a taxi. I slowly accepted all this and found the Occupational Therapist a very amiable and happy character. He introduced me to tools again - I had used tools all my life. This was terribly hard as I couldn't even knock a nail into a piece of wood. Ooooh, what's wrong with me, I thought. I very slowly progressed but any effort would cause me to shake and perspire and my stamina would take a dive. Not understanding, my occupational therapist would say "you are doing so well". I thought "Am I? I don't think so". It was all so difficult.

I was building a bird box (oh, for goodness sake, I had renovated four houses in the past). However, as always, I persevered and found my O.T. such good company and he helped me along a great deal.

By train -

After many months, it was decided that I would be taken to the train station and take the train to Gloucester for occupational therapy. Well, this was an impossible task. At first, for many weeks, I was taken to the train station just to look around and get the feel of the place. I was just so frightened of anything, my confidence was nil. Then came the morning when I was to get the train. It was a mammoth task and one I couldn't comprehend. My son picked me up at home and I thought we were late, so this was bad news for me and I was in quite a state by the time we arrived at the station.

The train pulled in and I was put on it. I cannot begin to describe how terrible this was for me. I was panic stricken, frightened, just a lost soul. As the train pulled out, I was gazing at my son on the platform, in total fear. I wished the train would stop and let me off. I arrived at Gloucester station and my O.T. was there to meet me. Oh, was it good to see him. This continued for some time but I wasn't improving with these trips. The noise, the movement of the train and the people was all too much for me to bear.

Then the O.T. came up with the idea of me having a walkman. This proved to be the remedy. As soon as I was moving, I would turn it on and listen to music. This took the noise of the train away and also took my mind off the flashing objects as we sped along.

This was better and I slowly settled into my weekly trips. The O.T. would take me to a café for breakfast - again this frightened me. I would have to sit looking at the wall where there was no activity, not into the café itself, but my O.T. persevered and I began to enjoy it. Sunglasses were also suggested by him. It worked, and still does. It shuts people out.

I was put under the care of another Occupational Therapist, a lady, and I was seen by her quite often. I felt she was a great help to me and I was always relaxed with her - she seemed to understand me - perhaps a lot more than I did myself.

My first D.I.Y.-

The first summer arrived and, for some unapparent reason, I decided to try and remedy the problem of a large pool of water which gathered outside my front door when it rained. This was to consist of a gutter type drain, then a pipe to a soak away. I wanted to undertake this little project, perhaps I had acquired some confidence with learning to use a few tools again, I don't know. A student, who was on holiday, was going to help me.

We started. I would sit outside with a tablespoon which I used to dig the ground, slowly filling a bucket which my student friend would then empty. This contract went on all summer long. It was a very slow process but, finally, we were ready to put the gutter in with cement. The lad mixed it all and then we both laid it. Two buckets full, we fussed and fiddled until we hoped we had got it right. This done, we then went to work on the soak away. Once again, there were many bucketfuls dug out with my tablespoon.

After many, many hours of work, it was finally ready and the student gathered stones to fill it. The pipe was laid and connected to the gutter. Then for the big test - we used the hosepipe - and everything worked and still works to this day. **A job that would normally have taken me two days to complete, took me all summer, with help.** However, I did get a wonderful sun tan whilst I was working!

I'm a 'stepper' -

The brain injury department had worked out that instead of climbing steadily, I was a 'stepper'. This means I would go along on a horizontal line then, for no apparent reason, I would step up. For example, I was unable to cook, make a cup of tea, then just instantly that would change. I could boil a kettle, I could make a cup of tea. I would then realise that there were other things that went with this 'step up'. (This has continued ever since my injury).

Life went on. However, I was still looking out from my world...... to your world.......

I was walking a lot better by this time and didn't fall over very much when I wasn't dizzy, but I still had constant ringing in my ears (which is still with me today). I had mentioned to my O.T. that I had always been a good swimmer, so they arranged for a lady from a voluntary group to call and discuss this with me.

Learning how to swim again-

As I still had no short term memory, I would write everything down. So it was written that someone from 'Lifestyles' was going to call to discuss with me how to go about this. The day arrived and I didn't want anybody to come, but a lady did arrive - and she was late (the lateness was to continue which always annoyed me). However, she seemed a very nice lady and we sat and chatted. Then, totally out of the blue, she said "have you got your swimming things?" Panic stricken I said "yes" and before I knew it she was loading me into her car and we were off to the swimming pool. The car journey was quite traumatic for me as I felt she was flying along.

Arriving at the pool, I was most reluctant to go into the changing rooms but, with persuasion, this was accomplished and, finally, I was at the pool edge. I didn't like that one little bit, the ripples on the water were just unbearable. Again, with a lot of persuasion, I was led down the steps between two people and, slowly, walked along the side of the pool. It wasn't nice, I was very frightened, unable to look at the water, unable to enjoy any part of this exercise - but I knew I had to do it.

Finally, we reached the other side and what a relief that was. The lady was there for me and I am sure now was rooting for me, but probably not understanding just how I was feeling. I seemed to just go along with it, maybe thinking "one day I will be able to swim again". Back to the changing room, dressed, I was taken home, to sleep….sleep…sleep.

In between all this, I saw different consultants. Some I managed well, some I didn't.

My physiotherapy continued. To me it was wonderful. I was trying to rebuild my body and although it was a very slow process, I was beginning to get there, even though I couldn't see it. My old friend would pick me up and take me to physio, wait for an hour and then take me home. He is a good friend and, now, I can appreciate all he did for me.

I was taken back to Occupational Therapy again at Gloucester Royal hospital. My O.T. was overjoyed that I had made it to the pool. I wasn't that impressed - I thought to myself "here is a man who would swim 30 lengths once a week and they are delighted"! Then my O.T. explained. Apparently, 80% of head injury patients never go near water again. (Nowadays I can understand her delight, but at the time, I couldn't).

Life carried on and my trips to the pool continued, very reluctantly at first but at least I was leaving my prison that once I called home. I can't say when I started to enjoy my trips out but, after a while, I actually looked forward to them. My helper was always late and I didn't like this and even with all my frustration and moaning, nothing changed. I wouldn't recognise that she had other things to do apart from helping me. These days, years on, I can see it, but at the time I couldn't. I thought I was her priority and I couldn't contain my frustration at her bad timekeeping.

She appeared one day with a flotation thing - I thought cynically "oh yes, very impressive". However, she managed to convince me to wear it in the pool - it worked! My confidence started to return.

My new helper/friend

After about a year, my lady helper asked me if I would mind if someone else took me on. Oh dear, this threw me, change wasn't good for me. However, she was very persuasive and I agreed. I was introduced to a man who seemed very nice. He won me over straight away as he was punctual! He has since told me that when he applied to 'Lifestyles' he had told them he couldn't swim - he had almost drowned whilst on holiday and had been saved by his nephew. My lady helper landed him with me!! I was his first swimming patient. (I didn't realise it at the time, but he would only swim in his depth where he could put his feet on the bottom - now he tells me!!)

He was always on time, but would still find me pacing up and down by the gate and I would moan about how late my previous helper had always been. Driving to the pool, I would talk him through a bend as I used to ride my bike. When at the pool, we would get changed and with arm bands on and the flotation pad tied on, we would go into the pool. I still didn't like the noise, or the reflection of the lights on the water. My helper told me that if I went to the deep-end, then my life would be in the hands of the attendant.

After a few weeks, the floatation pad was discarded, then the arm bands went. My helper's confidence was obviously coming back fast, as was mine. I would go through the showers ok, then we went to a store for bacon butties - even better! We both enjoyed these visits very much. I didn't find it easy to walk through the store, again too many people, however I would, according to my helper, charm the waitress hoping for more bacon in my roll. I would take as many sachets of sauce, mustard, sugar that I could fit into my pockets. Why, I don't know, as I couldn't taste anything. (On reflection perhaps that was just a little hint in my brain of what I would do when I was biking and camping in Alaska).

We still had to sit facing the wall in the store café, so that I wasn't bothered by shoppers passing by. I would notice everything where I sat - if a crack had appeared in a wall tile that wasn't there the previous week, I would notice it, or if a table had been moved - all quite weird. By the time we got back home, I would be very tired, wander in and straight to my 'prison' bed.

It was still difficult for me meeting people, seeing them again. My view of friends had changed and I couldn't face many of them. It has taken me a long time to overcome this feeling and still it isn't completely easy. I believe that without my Lifestyles helper and our trips out, my progress would have been much slower. He was doing a job but I thought of him as a friend, and still do. I hope he feels the same. I have also met his wife, who I think has some understanding of how I was and how I am now. She, I hope, is a friend as well. I did spend a night at their home - it was the first time I had left my 'prison' after returning home from hospital. Once again, it was very traumatic for me. Apparently, there had been a plan concocted for me to do this - surprise was the plan for advancement - it worked! After that, I stayed a night at another friend's house, same procedure - again, it worked and now I have no problem with sleeping here, there and everywhere!

Occupational therapy continued and after some time I looked forward to my trips, the occupational therapist still meeting me at the station and taking me for breakfast, all which helped my confidence. I still couldn't look up in a café, always looking at the wall if possible.

I was still frightened in crowds, in case I was separated from the person I was with, and it was suggested I have a whistle with me. This immediately solved the problem in my mind - but I don't think I ever had to use it!

My woodwork continued and the bird box began to take shape.

My memory - what memory?

The O.T. was also a biker and we would chat about bikes. He would always talk me through my problems but for a long time I was saying "yes" to everything but within a short time, I had forgotten everything. However, eventually, bit by bit I would remember the conversation two or three days later - this hasn't changed much even now. Since my accident, over the years, there has been a slight improvement to my short term memory, but chiefly I have adapted to my memory problems and seem to cope very well.

When I went for memory tests, I would always say "there is a great improvement" but would then fall flat on my face. What I was doing was just adapting to my memory problem. My filofax was my survival kit. Also my O.T. lady gave me the idea of fixing a clip on the front of my filofax, where I could put my notes for the day. If I could read my notes, then a job would get done - if I didn't see it, then things wouldn't get done. Also, I would start doing something, think of something else, go off and do that job. My son would sometimes find things I had started all over the house and then left them and not return to finish them unless I was passing that way.

It was also suggested that I had a timer with a bell on, fixed to my filofax. This was a great help for me and if I was cooking I would set my timer for a few minutes and then if I had wandered off, the alarm would go and remind me.

My life was very solitary. At the time I thought it was OK but it was actually a very, very lonely existence.

Walking - for pleasure?

My sorties then became a bit more frequent. It was decided that we, my helper friend and I, would try walking. My decision was to walk, if I must, to where I had always walked - the large parklands not too far away. The plans were made and my helper friend arrived on time as always and we set off, eventually arriving at the park. Boots went on and we were off - I believe I made the first one hundred yards then I had to return to the car - it was a struggle but we got back home where I slept. A good time was had by all?!! Perhaps, not the first time.

The next sortie was two weeks later. The same procedure and then the heavens opened, followed by big hail stones. My helper ran to the trees for cover, shouting "come on, get under the trees". "No" I said, I was still walking. "Why" he enquired. I said "BECAUSE I CAN ". I was thinking that "just a few weeks ago I couldn't walk far, now I can and who cares if it rains, snows, whatever, now I can do it - many can't".

We set off for the supermarket, again dark glasses on, panic in my heart. Two teas and two bacon butties were ordered and still I had to sit looking at the wall, still unable to take in all the people and the movement.

Our visits to the supermarket continued, tea and bacon butties. We did our excursions to the park as well as the swimming.

Getting back onto skis

I carried on seeing my occupational therapist regularly and, some 5 years after my accident, I was asked about what sort of other activity I had been involved in before the accident happened. I mentioned skiing. There were a few looks exchanged between the staff and, before I knew it, the following week I was told that they had been talking to Lifestyles again, who knew a group who took people with injuries to a dry ski slope. They were happy to take me - oh panic again, heart thumping, but I knew an opportunity was being presented to me. So, a couple of weeks later, I was taken to the dry ski slope where I met people like me who had had accidents and also people who had other disabilities. I knew I wouldn't last very long on this first visit but I put my boots on, then the skis and I managed to stay out for half an hour. I had had enough after that so I was taken home and slept.......and slept.......

My visits went on for several months and I was determined to do well and pushed myself as hard as possible. Then, one morning, when we were all together, the Manager of the ski slope came over and said to our organiser that he had been watching me and could he "take me on". Our organiser said "well, ask him yourself" - and from then on I was under his personal guidance. He was a great chap and great fun over the next few weeks and he taught me a 'style' (anyone who skis knows that to have a style, i.e. doing it right, is of great benefit). After some time he told me I was ready and that year I had a few days skiing in the Alps and my 'style' paid off! I now go skiing every year and enjoy this so much. I still have to pace myself, i.e. quiet morning and then one - two - three hours of skiing - then rest. I feel I am back on top of the world.

Most of the time up until five years on from the accident, I was looking out from my own world to your world.........but perhaps, just perhaps, I was very slowly improving..........................

This was the long, slow road to recovery.

CHAPTER 40. BUILDING A CLAIM FOR COMPENSATION

Because my accident had been caused by someone else, there was to be a claim for compensation. This meant Solicitors.

I seem to remember I started off with a lady who was very good, but she became ill and had to pass me on to someone else. This was a man, and I couldn't stand him. He made me feel very alone. He was getting the better of me and I felt he was pushing me backwards. To my great relief I was contacted by the firm of solicitors and told that the man had left, so I was being referred to a senior partner in the department. Once I had spoken to him, I felt safe again and put great faith in him, which proved to be justified. I would like to think he is a friend - he is just such a nice chap. I don't think I was easy, but he seemed to always have time for me.

Obviously, I had to be taken for assessments for an insurance claim - after all, I had nearly lost my life, I had lost the ability to earn my living, I was a mess. Going for assessments wasn't nice, but I had to bear it.

The first assessment I attended turned into a very bad experience for me, with the consultant involved, appointed by the insurance company. I was left alone with her and found it to be very difficult. I think I was with her for one, maybe two hours. My appointment was for 2.00 p.m., which was normally my resting time. I couldn't change the appointment so, on the day, my son accompanied me to the hospital. I was already tired by the time I got there and my stamina was dropping. I was with a nurse first of all and did the best I could. I felt very tired. I then went in to see the consultant. It was terrible. She had a streaming cold and I had the impression that she thought that I was wasting her time. She told my son that I was not responding and getting things wrong. My son said "what have you done to my father, he's exhausted". When she finally let me go, I was in a terrible state. I don't remember any of the journey home, I was totally exhausted. I was put straight to bed, where once again I slept.....and slept.

It took me a while to get over the experience - it had knocked my confidence back, my stamina was low and my sleep pattern was all over the place. I now strongly believe that anyone with a head injury, or any serious injury for that matter, should never be left alone in meetings with consultants who work for solicitors or insurance companies.

After this terrible experience, I looked to the head of the hospital head injury team for guidance. He was great as always and approached the consultant I had seen. It wasn't a surprise to me that the view put forward was critical of my performance even though I had been put through a very uncomfortable experience for what seemed to be hours. However, my doctor decided to do the same process as the consultant had used. Doing it over several weeks, early in the morning and for an hour at a time, I passed with flying colours. My doctor contacted the consultant with his findings. The specialist report that the consultant produces can have a significant impact on a claim.

I also had visits from different assessors; one who worked for the insurers was fine at first, but my friend who was with me initially had to leave halfway through the meeting. The assessor's approach became more difficult for me and, yet again, I was given a very hard time.

Again, I strongly believe that this sort of interview should only be conducted when a patient has someone they trust with them.

It was quite some time after all the initial assessments took place when I had started driving again. My son had recovered my van from the farm - it was still plastered all over with my blood, as the pipe had thrown me into the van. I did think at the time that the farm workers could have washed it off, but, maybe, it was needed to be seen like that as evidence in connection with my insurance claim.

One morning I set off to drive to the hospital to see my father, who was very, very ill. I was driving my company van, as this was available for me at the time, when I noticed as I left home, a car parked at the end of the road with a man in who seemed very interested in me. I then noticed this car was behind me as I went through the village. Not quite understanding what was happening, I went down a few lanes, then slowed, and the car appeared again. I telephoned my son at work - I was in quite a state by now. He said "drive to the hospital and I'll meet you there"

I set off and I noticed that there were now two cars following me. I managed to get their numbers. I arrived at the hospital and one car followed me into the car park. Just at that, my son came in the other entrance and got out, walked to the car and asked "why are you following my father?". The driver immediately put the car into gear and drove out of the car park at a rate of knots. We gave the car numbers to the police and they confirmed they were from a private detective agency.

Again, it seemed very wrong to follow me to the hospital where my father was so ill and since passed away. I found it all very difficult to handle.

As time has gone on I realise why they have to follow all cases, including genuine cases. So many people cheat, or try to cheat, on insurance claims and consequently genuine cases have to suffer this procedure. I suppose the sight of me driving my company van would look suspicious to a private detective, even though it was a perfectly innocent situation.

CHAPTER 41. VISITING MY LOCAL PUB

Some friends in the village took me out and to a pub. Yes, this was fine, it got me out, I can see that now, but at the time, it was very traumatic. I didn't want to be there. I didn't want the people around me, I wanted to be back to my 'prison'. I got home and slept.... and slept..........

As time went on, my son would take me to a local pub for a drink and I could manage that. My preference in the latter years has been Guinness as even though I was unable to smell or taste, I still found my pint of Guinness very enjoyable as it's sour. I can only taste sour and sweet. So, I started to look forward to my excursions to the pub.

Gradually I went from one pint to two, then two and a half. At this time, there was a noted change in my character. Normally quite a passive person, I would turn into this aggressive man and not understand why. One evening, someone said something to me. It wasn't offensive but I didn't like it and wouldn't let up, causing quite a stir and upset. After two hours, the effect of the drink began to wear off and I realised what I was doing.

The next morning I emailed the head injury team at the hospital and immediately my doctor telephoned me. I explained what was happening and what I was doing, describing my fear at what was happening to me. I said "I will stop drinking", he said "No, that's not necessary. Tell me what you drink, how many and how quickly you drink them". I gave him all the information and he said "This is what you must do - have a drink but one pint, maybe two and you must drink them slowly, take your time then you will be fine. If you drink too much too fast, it affects the chemicals in your brain and the aggressive side, which we all have, raises its ugly head. More or less stick to the rules and you will be fine".

He was right. I know my limits and I stick rigidly to his advice. It works.

So now I have a pint and enjoy it.

CHAPTER 42.   DEALING WITH LIFE AND ONGOING PROBLEMS

As time moved on, my stamina still controlled everything I did.

Still problems with my memory - and ways of dealing with this.

My memory seemed to have reached a certain level and stopped.   I was often going for assessments and would still try and convince the doctors that my memory was improving.   I would do the tests and fail.

My occupational therapist said I thought my memory had improved because I had adapted to dealing with it.   Very slowly, with the help of my O.T., I was working out how to best deal with this because I was beginning to understand myself - not the person I was, but the person I had become - and it was difficult.   For example, if I left the house my lists were posted around the house so I would go through them - windows closed, shed locked, cooker off, fire off, but I would still go back several times to check them because I wasn't sure I had done everything.   I still do this today, but not quite as much.

At one time, I was outside and started the engine of my van.   I was distracted and went off forgetting the van.   I think the engine ran for four hours before it was found and switched off!

It was quite a regular occurrence for me to prepare a meal, put it on the cooker and start cooking it, then wander off and find something else to do, completely forgetting my dinner, then all hell would break loose - alarms going everywhere in the house.   I would then rush into the kitchen and try and rescue the meal I had started.   Many times it went in the bin - burnt offerings!

Again, I have adapted to who I am now and, if possible, when I am cooking I don't leave the kitchen.

Problems caused by my inability to taste and smell

I believe my cooking has improved but spending a great deal of time alone, as well as not being able to taste or smell, makes it difficult for me to know if I have progressed. I am sure there are regular failures, but I eat them anyway! I now find it very rewarding to cook and have friends over for dinner. They will always eat everything I place before them, which is such a boost for me. Perhaps they will sometimes say "maybe a little more salt" or "a little bit of such and such might help". This is good for me and helps me a lot.

One of my real dislikes before my accident was tomatoes. Now I eat and enjoy them (no taste!). However, I can cause serious problems to my stomach if I am not very careful.

I have always taken cod liver oil capsules, but I decided to take it by the bottle until my stomach complained. I told my doctor about this and he said he could quite understand why the cod liver oil was upsetting my stomach - I was taking too much without realising it.

Mustard was another wonderful addition to my diet. I found I was getting some sort of sensation in my mouth when I ate mustard and started to have it with every meal. Again my stomach objected, but I couldn't understand why it was so bad. I made an appointment to see my doctor and he asked me to keep detailed daily lists of my food intake, and present this information to him on each visit. He was always very understanding and would go through everything with me. About two days before I was due to see him again, one of my carers saw me spreading mustard thickly on a piece of bread, rather like butter. She said that that would " do my stomach in" - the penny dropped! Mustard was the cause of my stomach problems. I cut right back on it and my stomach was fine. I still find 'hot' things enjoyable, but have to be careful as anything in excess isn't ideal for me.

At one time, I became obsessed with cleaning. Cleaning the house, as well as ensuring I was as clean as possible. I believe that this was a legacy of not being able to smell anything so everything had to be clean. It became an obsession with me and I would wash morning, lunchtime and evening, thinking I may smell. My bowels also caused me concern at the time, as I didn't have complete control, so more washing.

Eventually, this all subsided, but I am still careful with self-cleanliness..

Physiotherapy

Life went on, in my world and everyone else's. My once home was still my prison. Living on a hill, I was unable to walk up it. If I walked down the hill I couldn't walk back up, so I still looked forward to my excursions to swim and walk, going to see the occupational therapist - and then physiotherapy once a week .

Physio was new to me. First it was an assessment and, once again, because it was new, I was frightened to go. Persuasion again won me over and I started to believe that some of the fight and determination I once had was returning. I liked my physiotherapist. My routine was set in a small fitness room and with her guidance I soon got into it and was enjoying it very much. Most certainly, this was making me physically stronger and, in the long term, mentally stronger as I was attending sessions, again seeing people who I really didn't want to see and talking to her.

The shock came one day when the lady who was normally with me wasn't there, so another physiotherapist was with me. She had no understanding of why I was there and I was unable to explain to her at the time - and I didn't try. This was normal behaviour for me, no confidence. She gave me the impression that I was wasting her time. I can now understand her attitude but, at the time, I couldn't. Physios are trained to be just that and do not, or can not, be expected to understand serious brain injuries. I found the next session was difficult for me to attend - just the fear that my normal lady wouldn't be there.

Learning how to do my shopping

So far as everyday shopping was concerned, I was having to take myself to the local supermarket. I would go and come back with very little, as I would panic, not observe and just wanted to be out of the place. As this didn't improve, my O.T. arranged to get me some help and a lady would come once a week to go shopping with me. She gave me so much confidence and then, after shopping together for some time, she would give me the list and just 'be there' for me, but not with me, just observing from a distance. This was hard but slowly I improved and found her a delight to be with and a very dedicated assistant. I have a lot to thank her for, as I have every one in her department.

Tackling mechanical repairs

One day, I decided I would change a headlamp in the truck which stood in my drive - necessary tools at hand, I started. After two hours of anger and frustration, it was done. I had sweated, cursed, struggled - and come close to putting a hammer into it! I felt I wasn't able to cope with this small job which should have taken me just ten minutes to complete. However, on reflection, it was another 'step' - albeit a small one! (Now several years later, I have recently changed another one - yes, in ten minutes!).

Going to the cinema

One evening I was taken to the cinema in a local town. The place was cold, I didn't enjoy the film, but I had achieved something else - a trip to the cinema. So, some time later, I decided to go again, but this time I would do it alone. I had a lazy morning, a light lunch, then set off on the fifteen mile journey. I got half way there and then turned around, got back home, into bed and slept. A week later, I decided to try again, same routine, made it nearly to the town but had to turn back for home again. Again and again I tried - and failed. Finally, after many attempts, I made it into the cinema, paid my money and went in. I was so exhausted with the effort, I slept through the entire film - but I had made it! Thrilled, I returned home and from then on, it wasn't such a problem. Now I work out my sleeping times - and try to see all the film! Another hurdle jumped - another achievement.

Travelling by air

It was three of four years after the accident when I felt that, maybe, I could get back on an aeroplane - another example of 'stepping'. I was

ALASKA – MY LIFE BEFORE ... MY LIFE AFTER ... A TRAVELLER'S STORY

fortunate to be able to email my consultant at the head injury department whenever I needed to, so I asked him for his advice on this next step - would my head explode, what about the air pressure, etc. He told me that when people first fly after a serious head injury, they do find it difficult. They can suffer with bad headaches during the flight and all the pre-travel stress and actually just getting through the airport is traumatic. He advised me to talk it through with my Doctor, just take a short flight for the first time, be well organised and advise the flight attendants that I would be flying for the first time after recovering from a serious head injury. He told me not to be put off and wished me good luck!

I thought about it and I knew I had to do it - it was another 'step'. The arrangements were made and I was scared, very scared. I thought my head would explode - but I did it.

I can travel by air now but I only fly to Europe so that the flight is not too long. I get myself organised so that I have plenty of time beforehand, but not too much as still, to this day, crowds of people wear me out. I have to be able to shut them out.

CHAPTER 43. A NEW LOVE IN MY LIFE

I became quite fond of one of my carers. She had walked into my home one day and said "Good morning, I am a new girl". Well, yes, she was tall, blond and very nice. Her nature struck me as most caring. As time went on, she seemed to be very attracted to me (why I didn't know!) but after some weeks of coming to me, I asked her not to call again as I had learnt that she was married. This absence didn't last and then there was no stopping us. She told me that she was leaving her husband. Not long after this, her husband came to my home, smashing a window, knocking me to the ground (I was still very weak at that time, so he could inflict injury on me) and then he caused damage to my home before the police removed him.

Once again, this situation was a very hard thing for me to deal with. I phoned my friend and he was there, almost immediately, and started to clear the place up for me. I then went back home with him and stayed for a few days to recover.

I eventually returned home and, thinking it over, I came to the conclusion that even though I was still very weak, I hadn't been too weak to have an affair with someone else's wife and when you play with fire.....well, there are obviously consequences to bear......

Some months later, my new love left her husband, moving into a flat of her own and spending more time with me. She had her job but, from the start of our relationship, I supported her. Her family was not pleased by this turn of events but, over the years, this gradually eased. However, one day, she was shouted at in the middle of a busy supermarket - she didn't know the reason why but the blame, I am sure, would rest on my shoulders. All these sort of events naturally put great stress on my lady and our relationship was put to the test on several occasions.

Life went on and when my love's father and mother became very ill, she nursed them both. She has a big heart, but her heart was not always for me then. I know why now. Unable to get the help she needed to nurse her mother and father, she eventually broke down and went back to her old ways. It was so very sad - her background and other people's influences on her over the years had caused her so many problems. Eventually, due to a number of circumstances, my lady and I parted company.

After six months, we accidentally met again, in a pub. We had a long conversation and agreed to see one another again (we all know that love is a very strange thing!). She had changed beyond recognition and moved on from her past.

I seem to be around number one in her life now. We get on very well and enjoy each other's company. Our love affair continues. It's just the two of us. I am now able to take trips to my home on the continent, but my partner is not a traveller so we spend a lot of time apart. However, this seems to suit us both. Her family is hers, not mine, so in a way we lead different lives at times. However, our time together is very precious - but my home is for us, no one else.

My family has always stood by us and have been great. My lady and I have come through some troubled times and, on occasions, things have been hard for me to take. I some times think - had I been fit and well, this would never have happened and I would have handled the situation in a totally different way. However, if that had been the case, I would never have met her, so, in the end a lot of good can come from a lot of bad.

Just recently, my lady and I were attending a wedding. She had a new 'Blackberry' phone and on the morning of the wedding, before we left the hotel, I was putting all her phone numbers into her new phone for her and I was texting all the people with the new number, on her behalf. However, when I got to her close family phone numbers, I asked if I should text them with the new number and she asked me not to. I turned to look at her and she was shaking from head to toe. I stopped immediately.

I felt I needed to write this chapter as the contents formed part of my long road to recovery. My special lady and I have reached a comfortable place in our lives now and, as I have said before, a lot of good has come from a lot of bad.

    Life is never your own, to share your life and love is life.

    If your love is not reciprocated, then you have never loved.

    Sadly, love comes not to everyone.

CHAPTER 44.   AT LAST - BACK ON MY BIKE

My love had always been motor cycling, but now this seemed to be on hold.

I was only a young boy when my passion for motor bikes began. This was inspired by a story I read in the "Motor Cycle Book for Boys", which was entitled "The Fourth Man" by Ixion. I was mesmerised by it - I was only young!

Very briefly, the story was about a champion motor bike rider attempting to win one of the prestige events at the Isle of Man T.T. Races. It set out all his meticulous planning, thinking, his knowledge of the bike and its intricate parts. He knew every single piece of the machine and what it was or was not capable of - he just wanted to be the one that won the race.

To cut a long story short, because of a brake rod failure, and the need to do some instant repairs on the roadside during the latter stages of the race, the champion rider came in fourth, but the thrill of his ride which he, and the crowd, experienced has stayed with me ever since I read the story and, indeed, it fuelled my passion for motor bikes in the years to come. I am setting out just a little bit of the story below, just to give a 'taste' of the descriptive passages the writer wrote in the "Motor Cycle Book for Boys".

"Ramsey he takes in one fierce swirl, which appalls the anxious crowd, just now speculating as to his fate. Nothing more menacing than the roar of his engine as he opens out past the hairpin has ever been heard in the Island. The watchers, dotted in the furze round the Gooseneck, gaze pallidly silent as he screams between the narrow, curling banks. At Keppel Gate and Craigny-baa and Hillberry, girls cry out as the ruthless, resolute figure dives down into Douglas, faster than ever man took that fell descent before. ...." "The last lap but one was a terror. Girls gasped to their men folk "No, I shan't look; tell me when he's past". By some fantastic miracle he survived every peril. He hurled his machine up to each corner, nodded into the eyes of death, wrenched the steel frame round at the last fatal fraction of a fiftieth of a second and crashed off hunting new perils"..........

"But when Bill hummed up to the pits for the last time, in one long, straight streak of incarnate speed and noise, his Manager repeated the all-out signal. The men in front had reaped their harvest of luck. No stops had slowed them. Their racing was tame by the side of Bills but, thanks to that treacherous brake rod, the inexorable clock pretended they were better men than he. And so the little black demon commenced his final duel with all the laws of time and gravity......".

Bill gained four more places on that last lap but still came in fourth! What a story that was, which has remained with me all my life. I love it!

However, even though it was now four years since my injury,   I would still just look at my bikes, that's all I could do. One day, as I was looking at them, I decided to take one off the stand and sit on it. I sat on it and it fell over with me. I couldn't pick it up, so it was left until my son came to see me and picked it up.

I couldn't ride - I don't know why - no desire to do so. No childhood story was inspiring me now.

Then, one day, I felt that I could - this was another example of me being a 'stepper', as the hospital had described me. I was on the road to recovery "motorbike-wise".

I phoned the local motorbike dealer and asked him to pick my bike up and service it. This he did and returned it on a Friday evening. On the Saturday morning I decided I could ride, but just to go and get petrol. Putting my bike clothing on exhausted me, I was so hot and tiring fast. But, bike facing the right way, off I went. Well....that wasn't so bad. I got some fuel and I felt I had never stopped riding - it all fitted into place. I thought I could do a little ride - two hours later I was still riding and it was then I noticed I was singing, something I had always done, but what was so strange was I was singing the same songs. For some reason, this hit me hard when I realised what I was doing. I was upset and pulled over, and decided it was time to go back home. I slept and slept....................

On reflection, nothing had changed, just an extreme lack of stamina. I was riding just the same as I always had done. Slowly I worked out the best times to set off for a ride - it depended on how I was feeling, had I eaten, had I had a good sleep. I would decide I could get to a certain point and then I must return. It worked, sometimes well, sometimes not so well.

Even today, some eleven years on, I still have to be very conscious of myself and what I do. I ride now on a regular basis, not long rides, but usually on a morning. Preparation is a good night's sleep, get up and get ready doing nothing else. Then off, just me and my bike.

I have just managed a four day trip with one of my sons and two friends, in the mountains of Spain.

What a lucky boy I am!

I have five bikes now, two new ones and 3 of my originals - they are like old friends to me.

I ride alone, as I always did.

CHAPTER 45. RETURNING TO THE ACCIDENT SCENE

One day, I said to my son "did I ever ask you what I was doing in hospital?" He replied "you asked every day". Obviously, I would then forget and go through the same routine the next day and so on.

I had always been friendly with the farm manager, even before the accident occurred. Apparently, he was devastated when the accident happened and even though he was seriously ill himself at the time, he came to see me at the hospital and, when I was discharged, he visited me at home. He has since passed away and I miss him, he was a good friend.

Finally, it slowly sank in that the driver of the tractor hadn't been to see me.

Apparently, the accident had upset him very much and after it had happened, no one could move him away and it took his wife to get him up and take him home.

I think, although I'm not sure, that he came to see me in hospital. If he did, what happened I don't know, I can't remember.

A long time after the accident, I seemed to have the need to see him. I kept wondering why he hadn't been to see me. I had no understanding of this at all. I didn't feel bad towards him, just wanted to talk, so one day I went to see him. It was very very hard for me to do this. When I saw him, he found it difficult to talk to me, but said he would come and see me. I left absolutely exhausted, got back home and again slept and slept....... I didn't blame him, I didn't feel he was bad, I just needed to talk to him - but unfortunately it didn't happen.

CHAPTER 46. MY OVERWHELMING GUILT

My life goes on.

Because of the accident, I wasn't a nice person anymore. I was angry, sad, frustrated, lonely, all part of what had happened to me, sometimes knowing, sometimes not, as usual looking out at your world, from my world.

I carry a great deal of guilt with me and this will never leave me. My youngest son, who was, and is, everything to me, probably suffered the most after my accident. I abused his loyalty, his love. He had taken on my business, looked after me. I would not have survived without him.

However, I didn't appreciate him. I would be angry with him, would shout at him, moan, groan, throw things, smash things. I am told he understood, but I don't think anyone could understand a father who turned into a completely different character, a father whom he had worked along side, who ran a business, was fun, daring, a friend - and had turned into this sort of person.

I will carry this guilt with me for the rest of my days - how could I not?

Having said all that, my life fortunately goes on. I did eventually come through a very long, dark and painful tunnel into the light. Now, instead of me looking out from my world to everyone else's, I am actually back in the normal world, hopefully a changed man from that person I was when the brain injury occurred and during the recovery years that followed. It took a long time, but my youngest son was waiting patiently for me, his father, to become as normal as possible - before the accident, friends would say I wasn't normal anyway!!!!

My son, like me, enjoys his motor cycling and recently we've managed a few days' serious biking in the mountains together, which was great. We also both like skiing and we had a holiday together in the Swiss mountains earlier this year. I think I am quite fit now but I have to work at this as my age is against me.

I consider myself to be a lucky boy...............

CONCLUSION
MY LIFE GOES ON

I believe this was a dream come true – I enjoyed every minute. My life has now changed in many ways. A lot of good has come from a lot of bad.

On reflection, my adventure was the experience of a lifetime. I would change nothing. Life is never easy, one has to work to accomplish one's goals. My adventure gave me a great deal of understanding and knowledge.

MY ACCIDENT

My life was held together by my children, family and a very few friends, some I have no memory of but at the time I sort of knew they were there.

The medical staff saved my life, the after care of the hospital got me on the road to recovery.

My youngest son took the full brunt of the consequences of my accident, but stayed with me and is with me today. How he coped with me I will never know, but he is just the best. There is great affection between us and I love him to bits. No one could wish for a better son. He has his own life now and is married.

My oldest son and my daughter have always been with me, if not actually by my side, but in my thoughts, I have a great affection and love for them.

My thanks go to them all. Without them I would not have survived. Thank you.

My Family, my old and new friends, my lady – I know they were there for me – and still are.

How can I conclude? I can't as, fortunately, my life goes on.

Mark Cheney